THE NEW FINANCE

THE NEW FINANCE
THE CASE *AGAINST* EFFICIENT MARKETS

ROBERT A. HAUGEN
Professor of Finance
University of California, Irvine

 PRENTICE HALL, Englewood Cliffs, New Jersey 07632

Library of Congress Cataloging-in-Publication Data

Haugen, Robert A.
    The new finance : the case against efficient markets / Robert A.
Haugen.
        p. cm.— (Contemporary issues in finance)
      ISBN 0–13–173080-0
      1. Efficient market theory. 2. Stocks—Prices—United States.
3. Capital market—United States. I. Title. II. Series.
HG4915.H383   1995
332—dc20   94–20508
                                                CIP

Acquisitions editor: Leah Jewell
Editorial/production supervision and interior design: Joan Powers
Buyer: Patrice Fraccio
Editorial assistant: Eileen Deguzman

© 1995 by Prentice-Hall, Inc.
A Simon & Schuster Company
Englewood Cliffs, New Jersey 07632

Printed in the United States of America
10 9 8 7 6 5 4 3 2 1

ISBN 0-13-173080-0

Prentice-Hall International (UK) Limited, *London*
Prentice-Hall of Australia Pty. Limited, *Sydney*
Prentice-Hall Canada Inc., *Toronto*
Prentice-Hall Hispanoamericana, S.A., *Mexico*
Prentice-Hall of India Private Limited, *New Delhi*
Prentice-Hall of Japan, Inc., *Tokyo*
Simon & Schuster Asia Pte. Ltd., *Singapore*
Editora Prentice-Hall do Brasil, Ltda., *Rio de Janeiro*

This work is dedicated to Professor Robert W. Mayer, who lived through the 1920s and taught me about the New Era Theory and the influence of Edgar Lawrence Smith many, many years ago.

CONTENTS

Chapter Three

THE ANCIENT FINANCE　　31

Chapter Four

THE PAST AND THE FUTURE　　42

Chapter Five

THE RACE BETWEEN VALUE AND GROWTH　　55

Chapter Six

"V"　　72

Chapter Seven

THE HOLY GRAIL　　101

PREFACE

This work makes the case for the *inefficient* market.

The efficient-markets paradigm is at the extreme end of a spectrum of possible states. As such, the burden of proof falls on its advocates. It is their burden to deflect the stones and arrows flung at the paradigm by the non-believers. It is their burden to reveal the inaccuracies of those who present evidence contending that the paradigm doesn't square with the facts.

Moreover, the case for market *efficiency* has been made many times by others.[1] In fairness to the growing number of advocates for the *other side*, I present here a comprehensive and organized collection of the evidence and the arguments, which constitute a strong and a persuasive case for over-reactive markets.

In the course of this work, I shall make a case for the following points:

- Players in today's stock market persistently make a fundamental mistake. This mistake was also made in the distant past, only to be rectified. Stock investors began making the mistake once again in the late 1950s and they continue to make it today. Those who recognize the mistake can build stock portfolios, or find mutual funds, which will subsequently out-perform the market averages.
- Owing to the mistake discussed above, the stocks that can be expected to produce the highest returns in the future are the safest stocks. Risky stocks can be expected to produce the lowest returns!
- Because of agency problems in the investment business, the opportunity that is there *now* is likely to *remain* there in the future.
- Once we accept the assertion that corporations face an inefficient and over-reactive capital market, many of the long-accepted principles of corporate finance need to be amended and revised.

[1]See most recently Fama, E., "Efficient Markets II," *The Journal of Finance,* December 1991.

ACKNOWLEDGMENTS

I wish to acknowledge gratefully the research assistance of James Berens and Jasmine Tingching Yur-Austin and the assistance of Valeska Wolf in preparing the manuscript. Extensive discussions and comments from Nardin Baker, James Berens, Michael Brennan, Laura Best, Naifu Chen, John Comerford, George Constantinides, Charles Cuny, Joseph Dada, Werner DeBondt, Harindra de Silva, Mark Fedenia, David Friese, Joseph Gorman, James Heins, Robert Holz, David Ikenberry, Philippe Jorion, Josef Lakonishok, Rohit Khare, Knut Larsen, Harry Markowitz, Robert Marchesi, Tiffany Meyer, Jay Ritter, Mike Rozeff, David Stein, Neil Stoughton, and Robert Vishny are deeply appreciated. Finally, my indebtedness to the "Tycho Brahes" of Finance, without whom I could not make this case, is gratefully acknowledged.

Chapter One

SEARCH
FOR THE GRAIL

THE SEARCHERS

For decades, finance professors in business schools throughout the world have tenaciously sifted through computerized data files. These files contain information on security prices and accounting numbers. The professors have been in search of patterns and clues as to why the market behaves as it does.

This search for the way things work has now paid off. The secrets of the market's behavior—the proverbial Holy Grail to stock investors—are rapidly unfolding.

And much of what we are seeing is truly astonishing. The results fly directly in the face of what has been called *Modern Finance*—the collection of wisdom that every MBA is required to master. We now see a market that is highly inefficient and overreactive; a market literally turned upside down— where the highest-risk stocks can be expected to produce the lowest returns and the lowest-risk stocks, the highest returns!

What we are seeing is so profound that Modern Finance is rapidly being displaced by something called the *New Finance*. New evidence is unfolding about what stocks are best to invest in, how firms should raise capital, how utilities should be regulated, and how CFOs should estimate their costs of capital.

Overwhelming evidence is piling up that investors overreact to the past performance of firms, pricing *growth stocks—stocks which are expected to grow faster than average*—too high *and value stocks—stocks which are expected to grow slower than average*—too low. Subsequent to these overreactions, growth stocks produce low returns for the investors who buy them at high prices, and similarly, value stocks produce high returns for their investors.

THE CELEBRATED F&F STUDY

Consider first the results of a study[1] by two professors from the University of Chicago named Eugene Fama and Ken French (F&F). This study was voted as the best article published in the *Journal of Finance* in 1992 by the widest margin in history! The *Journal of Finance* is the oldest and most prestigious journal in academic finance.

The F&F study spans the period running from the early 1960s through 1990, and it covers nearly all stocks traded on the New York Stock exchange (NYSE), the American Stock Exchange (AMEX), and the Over-the-Counter Market (NASDAQ).

F&F focus on the relationship between the accounting value of stockholders' equity (called the *book value*) and the *market value* of their stock.

Book value is the accountant's estimate of the value of the stockholder's stake in the firm. To a great extent, it is based on historical cost. You start with the accounting value of the total assets of the firm, and then subtract the claims on the assets which come ahead of the stockholders'. These claims would include amounts owed to suppliers, to the bank, to bondholders, and others. What's left is for the stockholders.

As I said, to a large extent book value is based on historical costs—it doesn't reflect the value of future prospects.

On the other hand, the market value of the stock *does* reflect these prospects.

If the prospects of future growth are better than average (growth stock), the book value will be small relative to the market value. Think of a company that has recently introduced a new and exciting product. The historical cost of its assets in place may be small, but sales and earnings are up,

---

[1]Fama, E. and K. French, "The Cross-section of Expected Stock Returns," *The Journal of Finance*, June, 1992.

and the firm has great prospects for generating even greater cash flow in the future. The market has valued the stock of this company highly. The book value of this growth stock will be small now in relation to its market value. The question for the future, however, is: "Will competitors enter the market with their own versions of the product with lower prices and smaller profit margins, forcing the profitability of this firm to revert to average levels?" If the market doesn't properly discount this possibility into the *current price*, it will be unpleasantly surprised as competitors enter, the stock price will fall, and *future returns* will be *disappointing.*

The opposite may be true for a value stock. Think of a company that is inefficient and poorly organized. Earnings reports have been poor, and the stock price has crashed, based on the assumption that the firm will continue its unprofitable ways. For this *value* stock, book value (the historic cost of assets) is large relative to market value. Again, the question for the future is: "Will the board of directors force existing management out, bring in a fresh team to reorganize the firm, bringing its profitability back to average levels?" If the market doesn't discount this possibility into the current price, it will be pleasantly surprised as the firm becomes more efficient, the stock price will rise, and future returns will be surprisingly *good.*

Remember. The Dallas Cowboys went from winning Super Bowls (growth stock) to the bottom of the league (value stock) and back to winning Super Bowls (growth stock again).

What goes around comes around.

In any case, growth stocks: *low book-to-market;* value stocks: *high book-to-market.*

And F&F want to know the relative magnitude of *future* returns for stocks that have *different* book-to-market relationships *now.*

They begin in mid-year 1963. Across the firms in their sample, they rank the stocks based on the ratio of book to market value. Value stocks on the top; growth stocks on the bottom.

The ranking is done at mid-year because they want to be sure that an investor that might have performed this exercise had access to both numbers (book and market) needed to commute the ratio. While today's market value is available today, book value isn't reported until several months after the close of the fiscal year. Presumably, by July 1 nearly all firms would have reported their book values.

Based on the rankings, the stocks are sorted into ten groups, each containing an equal number of stocks. The most value-oriented stocks are in group 1 and the most growth-oriented in group 10.

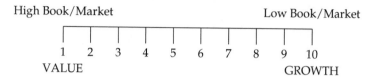

The groups are bought and held as portfolios until mid-year 1964. Then the stocks which existed at that time are re-ranked by book to market value, and the portfolios are re-formed in the same way that they were in 1963.

They, again, observe the performance of groups 1 through 10 through mid-year 1965. And the process is repeated year after year through 1990. The average annual return (1963–90) for each of the groups is plotted in Figure 1.1.[2] Take a good look.

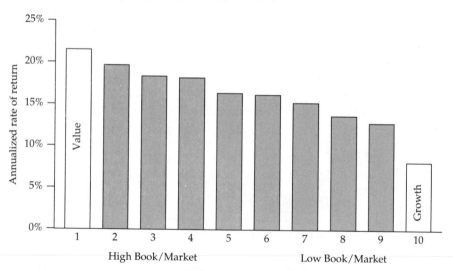

FIGURE 1.1. Book to market as a predictor of return

[2]The source of the plot is Table V from the F&F paper. Break-points for the groups are based on the yearly decile rankings of the NYSE stocks.

That's *21.4%* for the value stocks and only *8%* for the growth stocks.[3] And as we go from group 1 (most value-oriented), to 2, to 3, etc., the returns keep falling.

To be sure, each of the groups contains nearly two hundred stocks, and individual stocks migrate from group to group over time. Prospects change, and stocks may change from growth to value and even back again. But, for well diversified portfolios, the ratio of book/market value is an extremely good predictor of future return.

This is not to say that *all* growth stocks are destined to produce poor future returns. In any given year, the stocks in group 10 produce returns over a very wide range.

---

[3]Kothari, Shanken, and Sloan (Kothari, S.P., J. Shanken, and R.G. Sloan, "Another Look at the Cross-section of Expected Stock Returns," working paper, Simon Graduate School of Business Administration, University of Rochester) contend that the book/market effect revealed by F&F is due, in part, to the fact that the Compustat tapes (the source of much of F&F's data) contain a survival bias. The tapes were greatly expanded in 1978 to 6000 companies. The additional companies were in existence in 1978, however no companies were added that existed prior to 1978, *but not in 1978*. In another working paper (Harindra de Silva, "What Underlies the Book-to-Market Effect," Graduate School of Management, University of California, Irvine), the methodology of F&F was replicated on the Compustat tapes over the period 1982 through 1992, a period over which survival bias is not a problem. de Silva finds the following average monthly returns for firms ranked first by size and then by book/market

	Low B/M			High B/M	
Big	1.10%	1.19%	1.09%	1.29%	1.48%
	.50%	.85%	.99%	1.23%	1.15%
	.20%	.68%	.94%	1.13%	1.00%
	.61%	.87%	.96%	1.16%	1.52%
Small	2.59%	2.98%	2.77%	3.57%	6.91%

From this evidence he concludes that survival bias is not the source of the effect. We will get a better idea of the extent to which the F&F results are influenced by survival bias in Chapter 7, where we estimate the relative future expected returns to value stocks and growth stocks. A small part of the difference between the record of the past and our expectation for the future might be bias in the record.

Wal-Mart is a member of group 10. But its very high returns are offset by the low returns of scores of other growth stocks with great prospects that didn't "pan out."

DIAMOND HEAD OR DIAMOND BAR

Now let's concentrate on the meaning of the difference between 8% and 21.4% in the context of compound interest.

Suppose you're an investor of average means, and you're able to come up with $2,000 each year to invest in an IRA. You're 30 years old, and you plan to retire at 65.

That gives you 35 years to accumulate a nest egg.

How to invest the money?

You have a choice. You can invest in growth stocks (Portfolio 10) or in value stocks (Portfolio 1).

An annual return of 8% in nominal dollars is equivalent to an annual return of 2.47% *in real dollars,* given the average rate of inflation over the F&F study. This real return makes your nest egg grow to $109,232 at retirement (1993 dollars). If, in your golden years, you continue to invest in something that earns a 2.47% real rate of return (like growth stocks), you will be able to draw a retirement income of $2,698 annually without eating into real principal:

$$\$109,232 * 2.47\% = \$2,698 \text{ per year}$$

Good luck, and have a really *great* retirement!

On the other hand, if you invest in something that produces the returns that value stocks (Portfolio 1) have, your nest egg grows as in the rear bars of Figure 1.2.

Wow!

With a *real* rate of return of 15.18%, by the time retirement comes, you will have accumulated $1,839,369. If you continue to invest in this way *past* retirement, you will be able to draw an annual income of $279,216 in 1993 dollars:

$$\$1,839,369 * 15.18\% = \$279,216 \text{ per year}$$

Think of it!

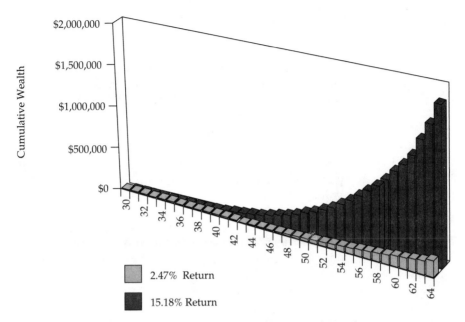

FIGURE 1.2. The roads to Diamond Bar and Diamond Head

For a 30-year-old investor, investing a mere $2000 per year in an IRA, the past performance differential between value and growth stocks can mean *100 times* more wealth at retirement, the difference between retiring in *luxury* or in *poverty*. This can mean the difference between retiring on Waikiki Beach in the shadow of *Diamond Head* or in the midst of the smog-filled San Bernardino Valley in an unexciting place called *Diamond Bar*. And even to live in Diamond Bar, you're going to need some real help from your rich uncle!

The New Finance gives you the opportunity to *choose* between going to Diamond Head or Diamond Bar.

WILL *GO* GO AWAY?

The Golden Opportunity *(GO)* of the New Finance isn't going to vanish before our eyes either. We're not likely to see massive amounts of capital move into GO, increasing its price and driving down its subsequent return.

Why? Because, as it turns out, stock prices are dominated by institutional investors (pension funds, insurance companies, trust and endowment funds). Because the fiduciaries, who run their portfolios, are subject to severe penalties for short-term underperformance, *they are and will be sorely afraid to take advantage of GO.*

These institutional investors are becoming increasingly aware of GO, but it's an opportunity they're very reluctant to take advantage of. You see, the performances of the directors of these funds are evaluated over periods of 3 to 5 years. So the directors, themselves, have very short horizons.[4] For stock investments, performance is usually measured relative to a stock index called the S&P 500. This index roughly contains the largest 500 stocks in the U.S. As we shall show later, in terms of total market capitalization (price per share times number of shares outstanding), it contains much more growth than value.

The performance of the S&P 500 is dominated by growth stocks.

Because these fiduciaries are likely to be fired if their stock investments fall short of the S&P 500 *in the short run*, they are sorely afraid to shun growth for value, even though they know this brings superior performance *in the long run.*

That leaves GO for us—the lowly individual investor. If the institutions stay put, and it is likely that they will, GO will remain available to us. If it continues to be, you won't need a lot of capital to get rich in the stock market.

$2,000 per year will take you to Diamond Head.

LOW-RISK HIGH-RETURN?

More good news. The road to Diamond Head is less bumpy than the road to Diamond Bar, because you get to Diamond Head by investing in the *safest* stocks.

As it turns out growth stocks are more risky than value stocks. Stock portfolios that contain high numbers of growth stocks have returns that are more variable from year to year. Much is expected from them, and the market is often unpleasantly surprised. Less is expected out of value stocks

---

[4]The use of relatively short horizons to measure performance stems from the fact that the changing nature of techniques and personnel in investment management firms make longer term performance irrelevant in assessing contemporary skill levels.

(much fewer unpleasant surprises) and, as a consequence, their periodic returns are much more stable.

Back to the F&F study.

We can use the results of F&F to find out if growth stocks really are riskier.

F&F measure risk by something called beta. Beta tells us the sensitivity of a stock's returns to changes in the return to the market index (S&P 500). Suppose a stock has a beta of 1/2. This means that if the return to the S&P were to go up by 1%, we would expect the stock's returns to go up by .5%. On the other hand, if the stock had a beta of 2, its return would be expected to go up by 2% or twice the increase in return on the S&P.

Beta, as it turns out, is proportional to the contribution an individual stock makes to the risk, or volatility in return, of the stock portfolio, or index, that it's computed with respect to. For example, if a stock has a beta of 2.00 against the S&P 500 stock index, the stock's contribution to the volatility of the S&P is twice that of a stock of comparable size with a beta of only 1.00.

F&F go through the same ranking process discussed above, but this time keying on beta rather than the ratio of book to market value. At mid-year (1963 through 1992), they rank their stocks by beta, smallest in group 1 to largest in group 10.

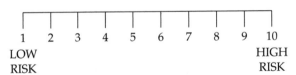

They then examine the average ratios of book- to market-value for each of the 10 groups throughout the 1963–90 period.[5]

The results[6] are shown in Figure 1.3, where we plot book/market against beta.[7]

[5]The groups are formed on the basis of trailing betas. The betas graphed are computed over the period 1963 through 1990.
[6]The source of the plot is Table II of the F&F paper.
[7]In this case stocks are ranked annually *first* by trailing beta (estimated over the past two to five years), which explains the smaller range of book/market ratios.

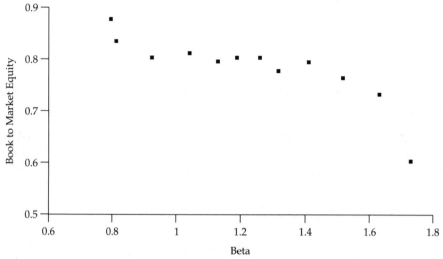

Source: Fama, E., and K. French, "The Cross-Section of Expected Stock Returns," *Journal of Finance*, June 1992, Table II.

FIGURE 1.3.   Book to market equity of portfolios ranked by beta

They split groups 1 and 10 into two subgroupings each containing an equal number of stocks. Group 1a has an average beta of 0.8 (very low), and group 10b has an average beta of 1.7 (very high).[8]

We don't need statistical tests to see the obvious. The high-risk stocks (group 10b) are the growth stocks with the lowest ratios of book to market value. The low-risk stocks are the value stocks.

The fact that growth stocks have high risk and low returns and value stocks have low risk and high returns brings us to one of the more interesting discoveries of the New Finance.

The riskiest stocks can be expected to produce the lowest future returns and the safest stocks the highest.

You can expect to get higher returns from public utility stocks than from airline stocks.

Gulp!

[8]The vast majority of stocks fall in the beta range of 0.40 to 1.60.

Chapter Two

THE OLD FINANCE

The old finance actually goes by the name "Modern Finance."

But it is rapidly being displaced by radically different ideas, so what was once Modern has become Old.

In the field of investments, the underpinnings of Modern Finance are contained in three basic concepts:

1. It is possible to build stock portfolios that have the lowest possible risk, given your objective for expected return. Call the technique to build these portfolios *The Tool.*

2. What if we assume *everyone* uses The Tool? Then, when we put together all our portfolios to form a market index, like the S&P 500, the S&P, itself, will have the lowest possible risk, given its expected return. This idea, based on the universal use of The Tool, goes by the name "Capital Asset Pricing Model." We call it *The Theory.*

3. What if, somehow, the prices of *all* stocks reflected *everything* that was knowable and relevant about them. This notion goes by the name "Market Efficiency." Call it *The Fantasy.*

There is nothing wrong with The Tool—other than the fact that almost *no one* uses it.[1]

---

[1]The Tool is used extensively by pension funds to determine how much is to be allocated to various investment classes—stock, bonds, real estate, and so forth. However, investment managers who build *stock* portfolios with The Tool are rare indeed.

This, unfortunately, makes The Theory a sham. If no one uses The Tool to squeeze unnecessary risk from their portfolios, the market index (if we put *all* of our portfolios of stocks together, we get the market index) won't have the lowest possible risk given its expected return. Better portfolios can be built with the same expected return and *lower* risk.

One of the claims of The Fantasy is that stock prices react to the revelation of new information very quickly and without bias.

Not true.

Stock prices *slowly overreact.* Investors overreact to new information about stocks, and they do so with a considerable lag. As we shall see, this makes it possible to easily build stock portfolios with much *greater* return and much *lower* risk than the S&P 500.

The Tool is cool, but be leery of The Theory.

And fantasies are usually gross distortions of reality.

THE TOOL

Modern Finance was born in 1950 on a Fall afternoon on the campus of the University of Chicago.[2] It began in the mind of a young graduate student named Harry Markowitz with the aid of Uspensky's book *Introduction to Mathematical Probability.*[3]

Harry was working on a problem which would turn out to be part of his PhD. dissertation. He was trying to figure out how to build portfolios of stocks with the highest possible expected return given their risk or the lowest possible risk given their rate of return.

What is the expected return?

Of a $1 lottery ticket?

Two possible outcomes: (a) $10 million; (b) nothing.

Odds: (a) 1 in 20 million; (b) the rest.

[2]True story.
[3]Uspensky, J., *Introduction to Mathematical Probability*, (McGraw-Hill, 1937).

Expected outcome:

$$\$10 \text{ million} * 1/20 \text{ million} = 50 \text{ cents.}$$

Expected return:

$$(50 \text{ cents}-\$1) / \$1.00 = -50\%$$

Not good, but let's face it. We're paying for the slim hope of becoming wealthy.

Stocks generally have higher expected returns—some as low as 5%; some as high as 25%.

Early into that Fall afternoon, Harry discovered that the expected return to a portfolio of stocks is an average of the returns to the stocks themselves. Of course, you need to weight the average by the amount you invest in each stock.

Two stocks—one with an expected return of 10%; the other 20%—invest 1/3 of your money in the first; 2/3 in the second.

The expected return to the portfolio is:

$$1/3 * 10\% + 2/3 * 20\% = 16.67\%$$

That was easy, but by 3:00 p.m. he had accomplished something more difficult. Harry figured out how to calculate the *risk* of a stock portfolio.

Risk: the chances of getting returns different from your expectation.

Also risk: the variability of your return from day to day, from month to month, and from year to year.

AT&T: low risk; Continential Airlines: high risk.

Harry found that the risk of a portfolio wasn't as easy to calculate as the expected return. Portfolio risk depends not only on the volatility of the stocks within, but also on how they move relative to each other.

Corn needs lots of rain; artichokes don't. Plant corn on the East 40 and artichokes on the West, and you'll get some kind of crop no matter what.

An increase in the price of oil is good for Exxon, but bad for Continental. Buy both and you won't care if oil goes up or down.

A low-risk stock portfolio is well diversified. It contains many stocks whose prices are driven by many *different* forces—oil, weather, exchange rates, etc.

Harry now knew how to compute the risk and expected return to stock portfolios.

But how to find the best portfolios?

By 4:00 p.m. on that Fall afternoon, Harry figured out how to squeeze out the greatest possible amount of risk from a stock portfolio.

Consider Figure 2.1, which plots expected return against risk. The little dots represent the risk and expected return of individual stock investments. Suppose you want a 10% expected return for your portfolio. Some of the individual stocks qualify, but they have high risk.

Harry figured out how to combine the stocks to drive risk all the way down to the big dot—the lowest-risk combination given an expected return objective (here 10%).

By doing this repeatedly for different return objectives, we can find what MBAs call the *efficient set,* which is depicted in Figure 2.2. These are the portfolios with lowest risk, given return and highest return, given risk (From now on, we will call the efficient set "the bullet.")

Forty years later, Harry would win the Nobel Prize. Not a bad afternoon's work, I'd say.

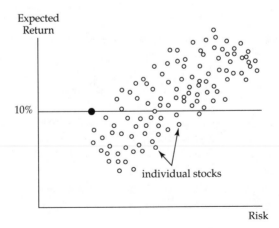

FIGURE 2.1. Lowest-risk portfolio with a 10% return

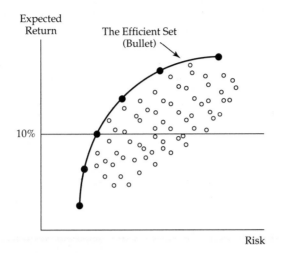

FIGURE 2.2. The Bullet

THE THEORY

The idea behind The Theory is simple. What would the stock market be like if we *all* used The Tool?

About 10 years after the discovery of The Tool, Bill Sharpe (Stanford), John Lintner (Harvard), and Jan Mossin (Bergen) simultaneously, and independently, asked themselves that same question, "What if we *all* used The Tool?"[4]

By 1990 Lintner and Mossin were deceased, so only Sharpe got the Nobel Prize for coming up with The Theory.

The Theory sees us all taking positions on the efficient set, as in Figure 2.3a. The big dots represent the positions of our portfolios. (I haven't drawn them for all of us.)

It's important to understand that, for The Theory to work, *all* the big dots must be on the efficient set.

---

[4]Lintner, J., "The Valuation of Risk Assets and the Selection of Risky Investments on Stock Portfolios and Capital Budgets," *Review of Economics and Statistics,* February 1965; Mossin, J., "Equilibrium in a Capital Market," *Econometrica,* October 1966; and Sharpe, W. F., "Capital Asset Prices: A Theory of Market Equilibrium," *Journal of Finance,* September 1964.

We must *all* use The Tool.[5] (Did you know you were supposed to be using The Tool?)

If we do, then when the dots are added up to form the market index (as in Figure 2.3b), the index itself will be efficient (lowest possible risk given its expected return).

The Theory predicts that the market index is an efficient investment. If even *some* of the big dots are inside the efficient set, the market index will be as well.

Do we all use The Tool?

Don't you remember when you were a teenager? Coming home late from a date. Trying to sneak in through the back door only to find your parents still up. Waiting for you? Nah. Instead, they were still struggling to figure out where they should position themselves on The Bullet for the next month.

Don't you remember?

Or the long talks on the phone with your Granny? Her words filled with her deep concerns about the peculiar shape of The Bullet this month, and what she should do about it?

Remember?

Okay. So we don't use The Tool, but surely the *pros* must.

---

[5]In the context of The Tool, The Theory predicts that the cap-weighted market portfolio be on what Markowitz called the *critical line*. (The line showing the stock investments needed to build a portfolio on the bullet.) *Other than by sheer chance, the only way we can expect that this will be true is if **all** investors hold portfolios that are also positioned somewhere on the critical line.* This being the case, when we aggregate, the market portfolio will also be on the line. The Theory is unique in this respect because its corner-stone is the predicted efficiency of the cap-weighted market portfolio. Advocates of CAPM can't lean on the notion that its predictions will be enforced by rational traders buying and selling at the margin. These traders have no incentive to trade so as to make the aggregate market index mean-variance efficient. Suppose all investors hold mean-variance efficient portfolios except for my grandmother, who for reasons of her own, chooses to hold a one-stock portfolio (AT&T). Rational traders still have an incentive to assume positions on the critical line. My grandmother's holdings of AT&T (off the line) are nevertheless aggregated, along with the others, to form the market portfolio. Rational traders have no incentive to prevent my grandmother from spoiling CAPM's central prediction.

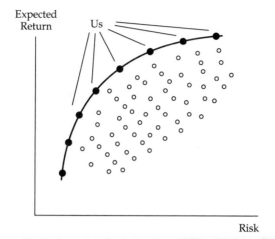

FIGURE 2.3. **A. Us on the skin of The Bullet.**

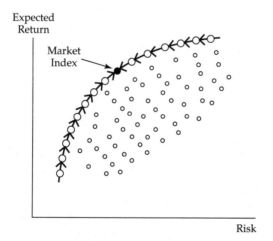

FIGURE 2.3. **B. We all make the market index.**

Do *they* use The Tool?

Sorry, Harry. You'd have to look for a long, long time before you'd find a single money manager using The Tool to help build his or her stock portfolio.[6]

---

[6]Some of the more quantitative managers do use what are called factor models to help them manage the potential for their portfolios to deviate from their benchmarks (usually the S&P 500). But these managers aren't attempting to minimize portfolio risk as The Theory defines it.

You see, *stock managers don't care much about risk.* To see this consider the big difference between the behavior of bond managers and stock managers.

Bond managers are very concerned about risk. They know the average grade or quality rating of the bonds in their portfolio. They are very aware of the maturity of their bonds, and their price sensitivity to changes in interest rates. In bond management *risk* is the name of the game.

But what's risk to a stock manager? To them *maximum return* is the name of the game. They give scant attention to the quality ratings of their stocks.

The pros aren't trying for the efficient set either.

Almost *none* of them are.

The Theory assumes they *all* are. *Us* included.

And in spite of the rather obvious fact that literally none of us actually attempt to hold portfolios positioned on the bullet, one of the favorite pastimes of finance professors is to run complicated tests to see if the prediction of the theory is true.

Is the market index on the efficient set?

Based on the results revealed in this book and casual observation of investor behavior, I don't have to run such a test to say confidently, "No."

Some professors have even gone so far as to see if the prediction was true in periods *prior* to the invention of The Tool.

How could we all have been out there using The Tool in 1950, and before, when it wasn't invented yet?

They *must* be joking.[7]

---

[7]In Chan, L., and Josef Lakonishok, "Are Reports of Beta's Death Premature?" *The Journal of Portfolio Management,* Summer, 1993, pp. 51–62, the authors state (in jest), in relation to the CAPM, "If anything, then, the model seems to work too well until the mid-fifties. It is possible that Markowitz's ideas were not so new after all, and the marginal investor knew how to form efficient portfolios long before Markowitz was born." However, the authors fail to control for size in their regressions. As we shall see in Chapter 6, this is crucial in a test of the relationship between risk and expected return. In addition, as we discussed in footnote 5, the predictions of CAPM can't be enforced by the "marginal investor."

THE FANTASY

Some finance professors still fantasize about a stock market dominated by an army of professional, rational, driven investors, who search in every nook and cranny for clues which might lead them to the discovery of an undervalued stock.

When they find a clue, they act quickly. Their trades push stock prices, making them quickly adjust to reflect the information in the clues.

Never mind about the trades of us "little guys" who don't have a clue. Never mind that *we* are driven by greed and fear. Our emotions allegedly have no impact on stock prices because "the professional army" is very effective at policing the level of prices in the market.

Many Professors hold on to The Fantasy with the tenacity of religious zealots.

Take a Zealot to the top of the Himalayas. Point to the fossilized shell of a sea animal, and ask him how it got there if the world is only a few thousand years old.

Zealot: "Simple. God put it there to confuse heretics like you."

Heretic: "Sir, while I must admit that's a possibility, there's a more plausible explanation . . ."

Many are now finding "fossils" in financial data which should convince all but the most ardent of the Zealots.

THE SHORT RUN AND THE LONG RUN

A recent study by two UCLA professors named Jegadeesh and Titman (JT)[8] provides important insight as to how the market reacts to announcements of success or lack thereof by business firms.

First, JT classify stocks as winners or losers, and then they measure their *subsequent* relative performance.[9] Winners are defined as the 10% of the

---

[8]Jegadeesh, N. and S. Titman, "Returns to Buying Winners and Selling Losers: Implications for Stock Market Efficiency," *The Journal of Finance*, March, 1993.
[9]The JT study covers the period 1980 through 1989. Thus, it avoids the survival bias problem in the Compustat tapes. The study includes all firms on the New York and American stock exchanges for which the required data was available.

stocks in their sample which had the best returns over the *past* 6 months, and losers are defined as the 10% with the worst returns.

They then observe the relative performance of the winners and losers over 3-day periods within each of the 36 months of the next three years. In each of the 36 months, they measure performance for firms that report earnings in the month, and, for those firms, returns are measured only during the 2 days preceding and the day of the announcement of quarterly earnings per share.

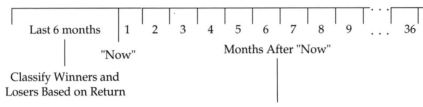

To illustrate, in the *first month* following the ranking of the winners and losers, JT would focus only on those which reported earnings *in that month*. For these firms, they look at the difference between the returns for winners and losers *only in the 3-day vicinity of the announcement dates (the two days before and the day of)*.

As we see in Figure 2.4A, where we are plotting the monthly differences in the return between the winners and losers, the winners of the past do better in the 1st month following "now"[10] and also in the 7 months that follow.[11]

Apparently, the market is being pleasantly surprised by the earnings reports of the winners during these months and unpleasantly surprised by the losers.[12]

---

[10]There are actually a series of "nows," one for each year of their study. The results are then averaged over all the "nows."

[11]These results can be confirmed by some earlier results in the accounting literature. See, for example, Bernard, V. and J. K. Thomas, "Post-earning-announcement Drift: Delayed Price Response or Risk Premium," *Journal of Accounting Research*, (1989{Supplement} pp. 1–36); Bernard, V. and J. K. Thomas, "Evidence that Stock Prices do not Fully Reflect the Implications of Current Earnings for Future Earnings," *The Journal of Accounting and Economics*, (1990, pp. 305–340); and Wiggins, J. B., "Do Misconceptions about the Earnings Process Contribute to Post-Announcement Drift?" unpublished manuscript (Cornell University, Ithaca, N.Y.).

[12]The monthly difference in "announcement day" performance is statistically significant at least at the 5% level for months 1 through 7.

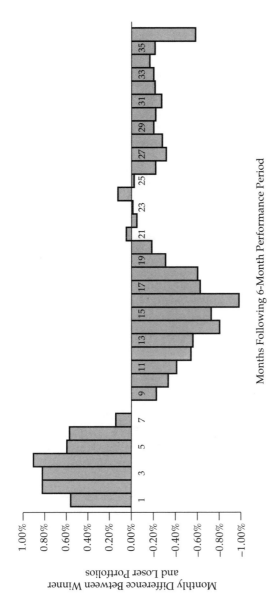

Months Following 6-Month Performance Period

Source: Jegadeesh, N., and S. Titman, "Returns to Buying Winners and Selling Losers: Implications for Market Efficiency," *Journal of Finance*, Vol. 48, No. 1, Table IX.

FIGURE 2.4. A. Monthly difference between winner and loser portfolios at announcement dates.

The winners probably reported good earnings in the trailing 6-month period, the losers bad. We speak of good and bad relative to market expectations, so these are market "surprises."

The market's surprises in the 8 months that follow the trailing 6 reflect its failure to recognize that good quarterly reports foretell of a *few* more good ones to follow; and that bad quarterly reports foretell of bad ones to follow. The subsequent good or bad reports catch the market by surprise, and the winners outperform the losers as they are reported.

A rational, efficient market would be aware of this tendency. It would anticipate the good and bad reports in advance and wouldn't have to react upon their arrival. But look what happens after the 8th month.

Now the stocks previously classified as *losers* are showing superior returns at the earnings announcement dates.[13] Note that this tendency holds *consistently,* month after month.

Apparently, the market overreacted to its surprises of the 8 months before and the 6 months before that. The market became convinced that the string of good (bad) reports over the past 14 months were precursors of *many* more to follow. They *were* not. After the 8th month, the market is being pleasantly surprised at the unexpectedly good reports of the past losers and unpleasantly surprised by the past winners.

This is your first look at evidence pointing to the conclusion that firms quickly *revert to the mean* in terms of their relative profitability and the relative growth rates they report in earnings-per-share.

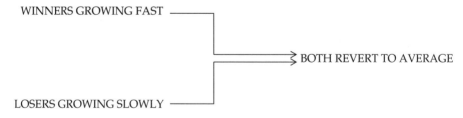

WINNERS GROWING FAST

BOTH REVERT TO AVERAGE

LOSERS GROWING SLOWLY

The good, as well as the bad, quickly become the average.

Some readers may remember the concept of the short run and the long run from Econ 101. In competitive markets, firms earn abnormal profits

---

[13]The monthly difference in the performance of the winners and losers is significant at the 5% level in months 11 through 18, and the losers outperform the winners in every month except 21 and 24.

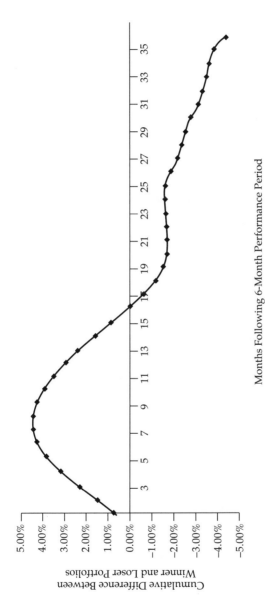

FIGURE 2.4. B. Cumulative difference between winner and loser portfolios at announcement dates.

only in the short run. In the long run, profits revert to normal levels. Competitors enter profitable lines of business, forcing market share and profit margins down. They *leave* unprofitable lines, providing those who remain with normal profits. *But they never told us the length of time separating the short and long runs.* A major theme in this book is that the short and long runs are *typically* separated by only a few years. The inefficient market, however, is not aware of this. Investors mistakenly tend to project a continuation of abnormal profit levels for prolonged periods into the future. The stock prices for successful firms tend to become overvalued. Unsuccessful firms tend to become undervalued. Then, as the process of competitive entry and exit drives corporate performance to the mean faster than anticipated, the overreactions are corrected. The stocks of the once profitable firms produce low returns. The converse is true for their unprofitable counterparts.

This pattern is apparent in Figure 2.4B, which shows the *cumulative* difference in the returns of the winners and losers. By the time we get to the 36th month, the losers have outperformed the winners on a cumulative basis.[14] This implies that the sum of the initial 6-month performance and the performance in the subsequent 8-month period was an overreaction that has finally been corrected.

The market overreacts—with a lag.

So what do the Zealots think of this fossil?

THE ENGINE THAT DRIVES US TO DIAMOND HEAD

The pattern revealed in Figures 2.4A and 2.4B is a recurring one that appears in the results of other studies. In the 6-month period during which the winners and losers were named, the winners obviously outperformed. But they *continue* their winning ways in the next 8 months that follow.

In the short run, stocks that do well have a tendency to continue to do so. Stocks that do badly sink even further beyond that.

The market failed to recognize that good news has a tendency to signal more to follow *just around the corner.* Failing to recognize this, positive price

---

[14]To obtain the returns implied by Fig. 2.4B, you would have to trade in the portfolio so as to be invested at the beginning of each month in the stocks that are expected to report earnings for the month.

reactions to the initial news tend to be followed by more positive reactions to the news that follows.

And the converse tends to be true for the bad-news stocks.

+ followed by +

− followed by −

Inertia in the short run.

But the sums of the ++ and the − − tend to be *overreactions*. And these overreactions tend to be corrected after the inertia dissipates.

The market overreacts because it believes that *a sequence* of positive or negative announcements foretells an *extended* series of future announcements of the same sign. The market believes that growth stocks will continue to grow, and value stocks will continue to languish. *The market believes that the long run is far, far away.*

This is a mistake, and when the market sees the extended series coming out mixed rather than consistent, it corrects the price, *reversing* the initial inertia pattern.

As we see in Figures 2.4A and 2.4B, the correction takes place over an extended period, but its magnitude is rather dramatic, and it truly is the *engine* that drives GO.

++ followed by −

− − followed by +

Inertia in the *short term*, followed by *reversals* in the *long term*.

We will get to Diamond Head by investing in value stocks. Today's value stocks have experienced the − − *in the past.* By buying them today, we get the + *in the future.*

Interestingly, we can confirm these patterns in stock prices by looking at *volatility* of return, where return is measured over different intervals— weeks, months, years, and numbers of years. Volatility is a measure of the extent to which a stock's returns can differ from month to month or from year to year.[15]

---

[15]Technically, volatility is the standard deviation of a series of returns.

Consider Figure 2.5. We plot two periods of time along the horizontal axis. (We'll define the length of the periods later.) Stock price is plotted vertically. The solid lines are consistent with inertia in stock prices—increases follow increases; declines follow declines. The broken lines are consistent with reversals.

Suppose we measure returns over one-period intervals (from 0 to 1). The range of possible return is the same regardless of whether we're dealing with inertia or reversal patterns.

But if return is, instead, measured over a two-period interval (from 0 to 2), the range is much greater if inertia is present than if we're dealing with reversals.

If returns have inertia patterns: increase the length of the return interval, and volatility should go up rather quickly.

If returns tend to reverse direction: increase the length of the return interval, and volatility should go up more slowly and perhaps even fall.[16]

Suppose the length of the interval plotted on the horizontal axis of Figure 2.5 is in weeks. If *inertia* is present in stock prices in the short term (over

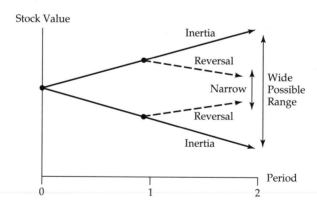

FIGURE 2.5. Range of possible outcomes with inertia and reversal patterns

---

[16]If we square the volatility we get the variance. If there are no reversal or inertia patterns in the series (if the series is random), then the variance can be expected to be proportional to the length of the return interval. The variance of annual returns should be 12 times the variance of monthly returns.

a few months), we should see volatility go up quickly as the number of weeks used to calculate the return is increased. With inertia, as we increase the return interval, we dramatically increase the range of possibilities for the return. If returns persist in direction from week to week, the return for the next month can be very large or very small, depending on whether the month begins with an advance or a decline. Advances feed further advances, and declines feed declines.

If, instead, weekly returns tend to reverse, initial advances or declines will tend to be erased by subsequent movements in the opposite direction, keeping the *monthly* return from becoming extremely large or extremely small (negative).

Let's see what happens to volatility of return when we increase the return interval from weeks to months.

Figure 2.6 plots the results of a study by two professors from MIT and the University of Pennsylvania, Andrew Lo and Craig MacKinlay (LM).[17] LM form stocks into three portfolios containing small, medium, and large-sized companies.[18]

The vertical axis plots the level of the volatility *as a percentage of what it should be if there were no inertia or reversal patterns present.*[19] The horizontal axis plots the number of weeks used in measuring the return. Note that as the number of weeks used in calculating the return increases, the volatility becomes increasingly excessive, relative to what it should be in the noninertia (or nonreversal) case.[20] This pattern becomes more pronounced as the size of the companies becomes smaller. Thus, the smaller stocks are characterized by more inertia than the larger stocks.

Inertia in the short term: The market does not catch on to the fact that a positive event is a precursor of a *few* more positive events to follow. A good

---

[17]Lo, A. W. and A.C. MacKinlay, "Stock Market Prices Do Not Follow Random Walks: Evidence from a Simple Specification Test," *The Review of Financial Studies,* Spring, 1988.

[18]Their study covers a number of stocks ranging from 2036 to 2720, depending on the point in time. All stocks are from the New York and American Stock Exchanges. The time period for their analysis extended from September, 1962, through December, 1985. Returns include dividends as well as capital gains.

[19]That is, if the series were random.

[20]All of the volatility ratios are significantly greater than 100% with greater than 95% confidence.

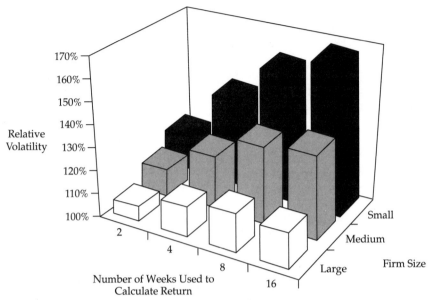

Source: Lo, A.W., and A.C., MacKinlay, "Stock Prices Do Not Follow Random Walks: Evidence from a Simple Specification Test," *Review of Financial Studies*, 1988, Vol. 1, Table 2.

FIGURE 2.6. Volatility relative to a series with no reversals or inertia

earnings report, for example, usually foretells of a few more to follow. Failing to recognize this, the market's reaction to the first report is incomplete. A complete reaction of an *efficient* market would reflect revised expectations for *more* good earnings reports in the next *few* quarters. There would be no need for further positive reactions in the next few quarters as the good reports come in as expected.

On the other hand, there is evidence of reversal patterns in stock prices when returns are measured over much longer periods of time.

Suppose the length of the interval plotted in Figure 2.5 is much longer, say in years.

If reversal patterns are present over periods of a few *years* rather than weeks, we should see volatility go up more slowly as the number of years used to calculate the return is increased. Strong moves up or down in the initial part of the return period will tend to be erased by reversing moves later on in the period, keeping the return over the total period in a narrow range. (This keeps volatility of return down.)

Let's see if volatility actually grows much more slowly as the return interval is increased to periods of years rather than weeks.

Figure 2.7 plots the results of a study by Poterba and Summers (PS), professors from M.I.T. and Harvard.[21] The basic nature of the graph is identical to that of Figure 2.6, but this time we are dealing with years instead of weeks, and we are dealing with different countries, rather than with differ-

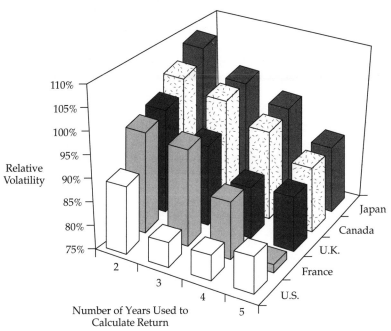

Source: Poterba, J. and L. Summers, "The Persistence of Volatility and Stock Returns: Evidence and Implications," *Journal of Financial Economics*, 1988, Vol. 22, Table 4.

FIGURE 2.7. Volatility relative to a series with no reversals or inertia

[21]Poterba, J., and L. Summers, "Mean Reversion in Stock Prices," *The Journal of Financial Economics*, December, 1988.
[22]For all countries except Canada and the U.K., the time period covered was 1957–86. For Canada the period was 1919–86, and for the U.K. it was 1939–86. All returns are inflation-adjusted and do not include dividends. PS test for the effects of excluding dividends in the returns by replicating the test with dividends on the U.S. and U.K. markets. These results show only minor differences resulting from dividend omission.

ent size groups.[22] Note that, in every country, the volatility is less than you would expect it to be in the absence of reversal patterns.

Reversals in the long term: once the *run* of a few positive or negative events materializes, the market develops a belief that the run will persist for *long periods* into the future. For example, if a firm's earnings per share have grown fast for the last three quarters, the market believes that this foretells continued success for many more quarters into the future. The price of the stock becomes inflated on the basis of this expectation. The market is wrong. Past success does not foretell of *prolonged* success in the future. As this becomes apparent *much later,* the past inflation in the market price of the stock begins to reverse, creating a long-term reversal pattern in the returns.

Considering the results of LM and PS together, we apparently have a market that is *slow* to *overreact.*

Chapter Three

THE ANCIENT FINANCE

GROWTH STOCKS WEREN'T ALWAYS

To continue this story, we need to move to a different place in time and space.[1]

September 24th, 1925.

Manhattan Island. Midtown. A curb on 43rd Street. Flooded from the morning's rain. Now approached by a speeding car. The right front wheel of which is about to displace a significant fraction of said flood. And send it hurtling toward a rather distinguished gentleman standing on the sidewalk.

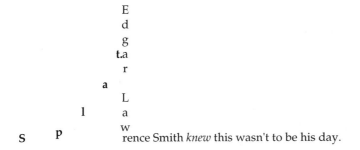

rence Smith *knew* this wasn't to be his day.

The '23 Pierce-Arrow sped through the rest of the puddle and down the street without even as much as an after-thought.

---

[1]While the following scenario is fictitious, the "statements" of Edgar Lawrence Smith reflect his opinions, as stated in his book.

Edgar now had the appearance of someone who had recently emerged from a morning's wade through the Atlantic. He beat his umbrella furiously at the coupe as it rounded the corner down 5th Avenue.

IMBECILE!

His fury wasn't due to the ruination of his trousers, as much as it was to the need of dry trousers to properly address the Harvard Economic Society.

In five minutes!

Completing his walk to the Harvard Club, he entered the building, walked through the reading room, which reeked of ten generations of securely settled tobacco smoke, and entered the meeting room where he was to give his address.

The room was filled with 50 or so members of the society dressed in perfectly dry business attire. He was immediately greeted by Jonathan Crestview, president of the society, and the man who had arranged for Edgar to speak.

"Mr. Smith, thank you so much for coming to enlighten us today. We're all very much looking forward to hearing about your book. . . . But what happened to you? You look like you just took a dip in the Atlantic. Shall I get you a towel?"

"I'll be okay. Sometimes I think we were better off with horses and buggies. Horses are more civil than New Yorkers, even on their best days."

To hide his condition from the rest, Edgar stood behind the podium and let Crestview introduce him from the side.

"GENTLEMEN! Gentlemen! Please be seated. We have the good fortune to have with us today Mr. Edgar Lawrence Smith, author of the much discussed book, *Common Stocks as Long-Term Investments*.[2] As you know, the book contains some findings and views that most of us feel are very, well, controversial. We now have the opportunity to engage in an interchange which should help to enlighten us all on these matters. Mr. Smith, perhaps you would like to begin."

[2]Smith, E. L., *Common Stocks as Long-Term Investments*, New York, The MacMillan Company, 1925.

Edgar spread his notes before him, and began with the tabulations which filled most of the book. Edgar had spent the last several years painstakingly documenting the performance of the common stocks and bonds issued by some of the largest U.S. corporations. He began with the year 1836, and tracked the performance of the two types of securities in various periods through 1923.

His finding: In terms of their annual rate of return, common stocks had outstripped bonds by a wide margin over this extended period of time. This happened, not only over the extended period, but also over most subperiods as well.

First confrontation. From the back of the room.

"But Mr. Smith. Surely, the wide gap in the returns between stocks and bonds was due to the unfolding of the particular events of the last 60 years. Had times been less favorable, the gap would have been much more narrow, perhaps even nonexistent."

"I don't doubt that, but notice that the gap reappears in all the periods in which return is measured."

"Are you seriously asking us to believe that such a gap can be expected to persist over the *next* 60 years? That's, quite simply, preposterous!"

"I don't believe I've asked you to believe anything of the sort. My numbers simply document what has happened in the past. You can judge for yourself what lies ahead in the future."

Now Edgar moved into what he knew was to be the most controversial part of his talk—valuing common stocks based on their potential *future* prospects.

"Let me now review the fundamental process which leads us to our estimates of the intrinsic value of common shares. As you well know, we must place principal effort in standardizing the numbers reported on income statements and balance sheets to reconcile the widely divergent standards applied by accountants in measuring the income and wealth of firms. I do not wish to argue here today over the means by which these numbers are standardized, for I regard these means as fitting and proper. It is not the standardization itself that will be the focus of my comments. Rather, it will be the *objective* of the analysis that will be my focus.

The fundamental underpinning of our analysis is, and always has been, the *current*, normalized value of earnings per share. It is also true that most of us modify this value to reflect any abnormalities we perceive in the current state of business conditions. We grope for an estimate of the earning power of the firm in a state of `normal' business conditions.

This number, normalized, *current* earnings, becomes the basis of our estimates of stock intrinsic value. To be sure, the multiples we apply to this number are somewhat different for different stocks, but the differences are currently based on our perceptions of the quality of the earnings or the relative risk of the companies.

I am before you today to state that there is another, much neglected factor in the intrinsic value calculation."

An initial buzz of excitement in the room. Then, quiet anticipation. A small puddle had formed at Edgar's feet.

"My results clearly show that a well diversified investment in common stocks may be counted on for a definite increase in principal value. But not all stocks have the same potential for this increase in principal. In estimating the intrinsic value for a stock, it is my feeling that we can quite properly consider the potential for principal enhancement in the future."

More noise from the crowd now. Much more. You might even call it a roar of sorts.

From the middle of the room a rather stout analyst named Bekker stood up. "Growth? Do you mean future growth in normalized earnings?"

"Why, yes. Enhancement in principal would be related to that."

Bekker: "That's heresy! We *all* agree here that future growth is a *speculative* and not an *investment* consideration!"

Edgar knew what Bekker meant. Investment considerations were things that you could predict and count on to some degree. Speculative considerations were basically the result of chance. Unpredictable.

Smith: "My results indicate that there *has been* a wide range of principal enhancement associated with different common stocks. It seems only reasonable that different stocks have different potentials for principal enhancement *in the future*. Those with the greatest potential should also command the greatest multiples."

From the front of the room: "And what evidence are you prepared to show us to support this contention?"

"The high returns on stocks relative to bonds result from the fact that the stock prices of the past did not reflect the potential for appreciation that was, in fact, to come. If the analysts of the past had taken this potential for future growth into account, stock returns would have been more reasonable in relation to bond returns. I'm simply asking us now to correct the mistakes which were made in the past."

After many more exchanges, Edgar, the heretic, actually thought he might be making some progress. But then he ran out of time.

Saying goodbye to Crestview, Edgar said, "Thank you for the invitation to speak about my book. Tell me, what do you now think about my views?"

"To tell you the truth Mr. Smith, I feel now as I felt when we first met today."

"Really. And how is that?"

"I do believe you're all wet!"

THE NEW ERA

By 1929 Smith's *Common Stocks as Long-Term Investments* had become a best seller.

Expected future growth as the underpinning of stock value had become the established point of view. A reasonable price, in relation to current normalized earnings, was no longer required for the prudent investor. Future growth became an *investment*, as opposed to a *speculative* consideration.

To see the change in standards, consider the following interchange from the "Answers to Inquiries" section of the *Wall Street Journal* from February 26, 1924.

QUESTION: Would you suggest some railroad stock to purchase. . . ? The idea is to buy something likely to appreciate in price, as well as to continue paying income.

ANSWER: We cannot advise you as to stocks which are likely to appreciate in value, since it is contrary to our policy to give speculative advice. The following are stocks that hold places of prominence as established earners and dividend payers in the railroad group: New York Central, Atchison, Southern Pacific, Chesapeake and Ohio, Union Pacific, Illinois Central, Baltimore & Ohio, and Atlantic Coast line.

Now consider a front-page article on the motor industry in the *Journal* on January 7, 1929.

Practically without exception leaders in the industry predict new high records in motor output for the year and continued prosperity for motor manufacturers.

When one looks at the (market) values that are being offered at this time, it hardly seems believable, yet I will venture to predict that with the spirit of progress that has prevailed from the beginning and still prevails in the industry, the end has in no sense been reached.

Or the following from the *Journal's* "Inquiring Investor" column on the outlook for Northwest Engineering, written on February 21, 1929.

. . . on the basis of the company's estimated earnings and outlook, the stock could hardly be said to be overpriced, and the matter of (dividend) yield would probably be adjusted through an upward revision in the dividend rate paid if present estimates of future earnings materialize.

As the general level of prices advanced upward in 1929, the spreads in price-to-earnings multiples began to widen dramatically. *The Wall Street Journal*, March 2, 1929:

It is evident that more attention is being given to values than heretofore. This explains the fact that many stocks have been moving ahead more rapidly than others. The issues representing industries which have been making substantial progress have been most favored. It is likely this tendency will continue.

Expected future growth became the modern concept, investing based on established performance old fashioned. Consider Charles Schwab's comments in the *Journal* on March 8, 1929.

Mr. Schwab says he no longer sees danger in the situation. "Last year my conclusions were based on old fashioned ideas," says Mr. Schwab. "Everyone has made money except the old timers."

Mr. Schwab merely repeats the views of many other old timers. As one remarked: "I have made nothing in the market for the reason that I got my Wall Street education 20 years too soon. The younger minds are not troubled with past performance. They do not remember the numerous panics and periods of stress as we old timers do. They are looking into the future. We are looking into the past. They have plenty of imagination. Our imagination is warped by events of the past. We made a mistake and will have to admit it, as Mr. Schwab has done."

This focus on the future by a new generation of investors is revealed in the "Broad Street Gossip" column in the edition of the *Journal* published on June 15, 1929.

It's not so much what a company is earning now as what average earnings will be in years to come.

This fundamental change in investment standards evolved as the entire country looked to the future with increasing confidence. Herbert Hoover spoke of the "New Era" in which cooperation in business, aided by government and guided by scientific principles, would lead to prosperity for the nation and greater freedom in all aspects of life. The new, modern investment philosophy came to be known as the "New Era Theory."

In *The Great Bull Market*,[3] Robert Sobel writes of it:

In the past they said stock prices reflected the present because the future was uncertain. Now, however, the nation was enjoying permanent prosperity; depressions were no longer possible. If you *knew* that a company's earnings were increasing at a rate of 20 per cent a year, then it was clear that they would double in less than five years if compounded. Would it not be wise to take these anticipated earnings into consideration? In the past stocks sold at ten times earnings. The stock which sold at fifteen times earnings in 1928 was, in reality, selling at less than eight times 1933 earnings and so was more conservative a purchase than it would have been a decade earlier.

Before the first traces of the scent of the impending economic storm were to blow across the shores of Manhattan Island, the *Wall Street Journal* wrote on August 7th, 1929:

Now we have come into the jazz age, and principles which have not been established by facts are ignored, they are subordinated in new experiences and more fruitful maxims. We may say that the deductive method of accepting certain stereotyped premises and investing strictly in accord with them has been abandoned for the inductive method of accumulating our own facts and establishing our own principles. This change has brought common stocks into high favor with special emphasis on companies which have possibilities of continuous expansion over an indefinite period.

[3]Sobel, R., *The Great Bull Market*, New York, W.W. Norton and Company, 1968, p. 119.

But as the "modern" investors of the late 20s were soon to learn, depressions were far from impossible. The New Era Theory was about to collapse under the weight of the great stock market crash of October, 1929, which served as the gateway to the great depression of the 1930s.

Later, in the midst of the rubble of the financial and economic debacle, two men, who were to attain great influence in the decades to come, wrote the first edition of their book, *Security Analysis*.[4] In this book they attacked the tenets of the New Era Theory. Graham and Dodd felt that future growth was largely, if not completely, unpredictable. They were particularly opposed to estimating future earnings by extrapolating from past trend.

Value based on a satisfactory trend must be wholly arbitrary and hence speculative, and hence inevitably subject to exaggeration and later collapse.

Their book was to become the Bible of the investment business. It evolved through several editions, but Graham and Dodd held steadfast to their views. In the 1951 edition, they write:

The analyst's philosophy must still compel him to base his investment valuation on an assumed earning power no larger than the company has already achieved in some year of normal business. Investment value can be related only to demonstrated performance.[5]

Graham and Dodd maintained their influence throughout most of the 1950s. But as the great bull market of the 50s commenced and marched onward and upward, a "new" philosophy began to emerge. Once again, the likes of Graham and Dodd cried heresy!

But the new philosophy again took hold—stock prices should properly be based on future prospects for growth.

Only those who put their ears to the rail and listened *very* carefully were able to discern that these *new* thoughts were merely *echoes* of the sounds made by Growth Train # 1, which had rumbled its way through New York Station some 30 years before.

[4]Graham, B., and D. Dodd, *Security Analysis,* New York, McGraw Hill, 1934.
[5]Graham, B., D. Dodd, and C. Tatham, *Security Analysis,* 3rd ed. New York, McGraw Hill, 1951, pp. 422–23.

THE RENAISSANCE

By 1960 growth stock investing was back.

As with its emergence in the 1920s, its arrival was not heralded by published evidence documenting that either (a) the "old timers" (many of whom were now the *children* of the young hot shots of the 1920s) were wrong about future growth not being subject to reliable forecasts or (b) the nature of the world had now changed and the relative growth rate of two companies could now be reliably projected for extended periods of time into the future.

No evidence whatsoever that either (a) or (b) was true was ever put on the table.

Some old, old timers did experience some *déja vu*, however.

Just as E. L. Smith's book preceded Train # 1 in 1925, a businessman named Winthrop Walker published a book in 1954 called, *A Re-examination of Common Stocks as Long-Term Investments.*[6] In it he extended Edgar's study to cover the period 1923–51. Walker concludes:

> Our prudent investor can justifiably conclude . . . that he can continue to hold his common stocks with the confident prospect that over the long-term he will enjoy not only greater income return than from bonds, but also a greater protection for his capital.

These results were to be buttressed ten years later when two professors from the University of Chicago published the results of a study of the performance of common stocks traded on the New York stock exchange during the period 1926 through 1959.[7] They found that, on average, the stocks had earned approximately 9% per annum—an extraordinarily high number, given the relatively low yields to be had on bonds at that time.

Although Growth Train # 1 was launched by Smith's single book which (a) documented the relatively strong performance of common stocks in the past and (b) suggested that current stock values should properly be based

---

[6]Walker, W. B., *A Re-examination of Common Stocks as Long Term Investments,* Grand National Bank of Portland, 1954.
[7]Fisher, L. and J. Lorie, "Rates of Return on Investments in Common Stock," *Journal of Business,* January, 1964.

on future prospects, the Growth Train # 2 was supported by several publications in which ideas (a) and (b) were offered separately.

A professor from M.I.T. named Myron Gordon suggested (b). In his book, published in 1962, he writes:

> In our stock price model a future dividend expectation is what an investor buys. However, *he is not considered so naive as to assume that every future dividend is equal to the current dividend.* He is interested in both the current dividend and its rate of growth.[8]

Gordon goes on to set forth complicated mathematical models designed to capture the determinants of the value of common stock. And the centerpiece of these models was the *future rate of growth of earnings and dividends per share.*

None of the publications attempt to *debunk* the old timers' contentions that future growth is speculative and not subject to reliable forecasts. Instead it seems that both Growth Trains came through riding the crests of bull markets.

Bull markets in which current prices could no longer be justified on the basis of standards which had been applied in the past. The general level of prices could only be justified as compared with the expected *future* level of earnings.

And if you were going to justify the *general level* of prices on this basis, why not justify the *relative structure* of prices in the same way? Growth stocks command premium *prices* because they have premium *prospects.*

As a happy rider on Growth Train # 2 in 1968, Robert Sobel concluded that:

> . . . price/earnings were unreasonable in 1928–1929 only when compared with those of 1920 and earlier; when placed side by side with those of today they appear sensible and even a bit on the low side.[9]

> To illustrate this point, we might consider the record of Radio Corporation of America, the greatest glamour issue of the twenties, and compare it with Syntex, a similar favorite of the post–World War II market.

[8]Gordon, M. J., *The Investment, Financing and Valuation of the Corporation.* Homewood, Illinois: Richard D. Irwine, 1962, p. 5.
[9]Sobel, R., *The Great Bull Market*, p. 122.

COMPARISON OF R.C.A. AND SYNTEX COMMON STOCKS
FOR SELECTED YEARS

Year	High R.C.A.	Earnings (share)	Year	High Syntex	Earnings (share)
1925	77&$\frac{7}{8}$	$1.32	1962	11	$0.14
1926	61&$\frac{5}{8}$	2.85	1963	67&$\frac{1}{2}$	0.47
1927	101	6.15	1964	95&$\frac{1}{4}$	0.91
1928	420	15.98	1965	109	1.18[10]

From Sobel, R. *The Great Bull Market*, p.121.

Both Trains were similar in nature and left the station with similar speed. *It took THE GREAT DEPRESSION to de-rail # 1.* Train # 2 is still on track.

Two points of view. Growth is reliably predictable. It is not.

The nature of the world does not change overnight. One of these views is closer to wrong, the other closer to right.

As we walk the tracks of the twentieth century, opinions evolve *dramatically*.

Heresy becomes truth.

Truth becomes heresy.

Heresy returns again as truth.

Which is which?

Let the evidence speak.

Chapter Four

THE PAST
AND THE FUTURE

HIGGLEDY PIGGLEDY GROWTH

Ironically, just after Growth Train #2 pulled away from the station, a British economist named Little was immersed in research that would buttress the conservative views of the old timers.

I. M. D. Little. (I'll leave it to you to figure out why Ian's parents thought he might need that third initial.)

Little was trying to determine whether the firms that grew the fastest in the past tended to repeat their relative performance in the future. In his writings, he repeatedly apologizes for even raising such a silly question. After all, isn't it obvious that the best firms of the past are, at the very least, going to be the better firms of the future?

Very much aware of the emergence of Train #2, Little writes in his 1962 article, "Higgledy Piggledy Growth,"[1]

My impression is that many stockholders, financial journalists, economists and investors believe that past growth behavior is some sort of guide to future growth. This belief seems to have developed especially in the last few years.[2]

And in his 1966 book *Higgledy Piggledy Growth Again* with A.C. Rayner,[3]

[1]Little, I.M.D., "Higgledy Piggledy Growth," *Institute of Statistics, Oxford,* November 1962.
[2]Ibid p. 391.
[3]Rayner, A. C., and I. M. D. Little, *Higgledy Piggledy Growth Again,* Basil Blackwell, Oxford, 1966.

Before launching into the investigation, it is well to start by giving some reasons for being interested in growth stability. The first is the one that the market is concerned with, which is that there has been, for the last few years, a belief in the concept of "growth stocks." For the privilege of holding these particular stocks, the investor has been willing to forego a considerable amount of income in the belief that their market price will rise in the future. This can continue to happen in a rational market only if past growth is repeated in the future. . . . Therefore, with this belief in growth stocks, investors are also expressing a belief that firms which have grown relatively better than others in the past will continue to do so in the future.[4]

Since the work in the *book* is more comprehensive, we will concentrate on *it*.

Rayner and Little (RL) study British companies over the period 1951 through 1961.[5] Again, they are trying to determine whether growth in the past serves as a precursor for growth in the future.

In one of their tests RL rank their firms based on their rates of growth in earnings per share from 1952 to 1956. They then form equal numbered groups, the fastest growing firms, fast, slow, and slowest.

Each firm counts equally within a group. The earnings of each group is indexed where 1952 equals 100. We can see the growth of each group from 1952 to 1956 in Figure 4.1. The earnings of the fastest growing firms move from 100 in '52 to about 190 in '56. The slowest fall to about 45.

The question of interest is: "Do the fastest continue to grow fast *after* the rankings are established in '56? And do the slowest continue to grow slow?"

No.

From 1956 on, the growth performance of all four groups is about the same.

RL find no evidence in this test that the future is linked to the past—at least in terms of growth in earnings per share.

Okay, maybe across a wide variety of firms there is little or no consistency in relative performance, but what about among peers within an industry?

[4]Ibid p. 1.
[5]Their study includes 441 companies that had complete records through at least 1959.

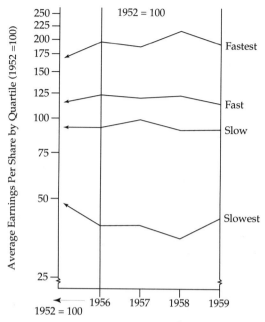

Source: Rayner, A. C., and I. M. D. Little, *Higgledy Piggledy Growth Again*, Basil Blackwell, Oxford, 1966, pg. 22.

FIGURE 4.1. Earnings behavior for fastest, fast, slow, and slowest growing firms (1952–56)

To find intraindustry consistency, RL rank firms in the same industry on the basis of growth in earnings per share in the first half of their period (roughly the first half of the 50s), and then they rank again in the second half. A firm's rank in the first half is plotted on the vertical axis of a graph, and the rank in the second half is on the horizontal. Each firm in their sample is represented as a dot on the graph. A firm ranking first in the first half and first in the second is positioned in the upper right-hand corner. A firm ranking last in both halves is in the lower left-hand corner.

If the rankings are perfectly consistent from the first half of the decade to the second, all the dots should fall on a line going from the lower left corner to the upper right.

RL's results are presented in Figure 4.2.

Wow!

What a mess!

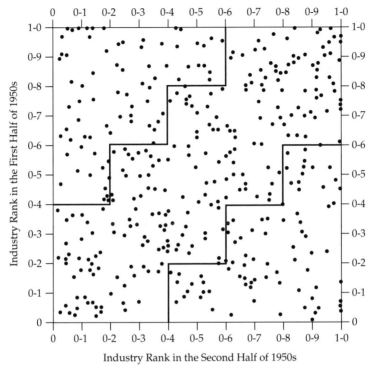

Source: Rayner, A. C., and I. M. D. Little, *Higgledy Piggledy Growth Again*, Basil Blackwell, Oxford, 1966, p. 50.

FIGURE 4.2. Consistency of growth relative to other firms in the industry

RL run test after test trying to find some evidence of consistency in the record. They find none. Finally, they conclude:

> Certainly investors are wrong to think that a few years' above average rise of earnings is evidence at all that good management, which will result in a continued rise, must be present.[6]

Future growth as a *speculative* rather than an *investment* consideration.[7]

---

[6]Rayner, A. C., and I. M. D. Little, *Higgledy Piggledy Growth Again*, pg. 64.
[7]Little seems to believe that the true expected growth rate in earnings per share is a constant across all firms. Observed deviations in realized growth from this true expectation would then be due to random chance. As we shall soon see, this view is probably too extreme. There do seem to be differentials in true expected growth, but true relative growth rates converge to a common constant rather quickly, because of the forces of competitive entry and exit.

HIGGLEDY PIGGLEDY GROWTH IN AMERICA

The results of L and RL attracted much attention, at least in the academic community. Was this peculiar to the United Kingdom? Was it possible that relative growth was unpredictable in the United States as well?

Two professors from Harvard, named John Lintner and Robert Glauber (LG),[8] took a stab at the question. (Lintner, you may recall, was one of the coinventors of CAPM.)

LG look at 5-year subperiods within the period 1946 through 1965.[9]

They are interested in explaining differences in growth in one period with differences in growth in the period that came before.

What percent of the differences in growth in one period can be associated with differences that were observed in the *preceding* period?

For RL's Figure 4.2, the answer to that question is close to zero. The rankings in the two periods are pretty much independent of one another. If, instead, the rankings were perfectly consistent (all dots on a straight line going from the southwest corner to the northeast), the answer would be 100%. All the growth differences in the second period could be associated with differences in the first.

LG conduct a similar analysis with U.S. firms.[10] However, in their study, *rates* of growth would be plotted on the axes of the graph rather than growth *rankings*.

Their results are presented in Figure 4.3.

The findings are very consistent with the results from the United Kingdom. At best we can say that only 1.7% of the differences in growth rates in

---

[8]Lintner, J. and R. Glauber "Higgledy Piggledy Growth in America," (unpublished paper presented to the Seminar on the Analysis of Security Press, May 1967, University of Chicago).

[9]While RL measure growth by taking the ratio of ending to beginning earnings per share, LG fit a trend line through the natural logarithm of earnings plotted against time. They take the slope of the trend line as their measure of growth. This number can be taken to be the continuously compounded rate of growth, where beginning earnings are given by the level of the trend line at its starting point, and ending earnings are given by their level at the ending point.

[10]Their study covers 323 companies with positive earnings during the periods of analysis.

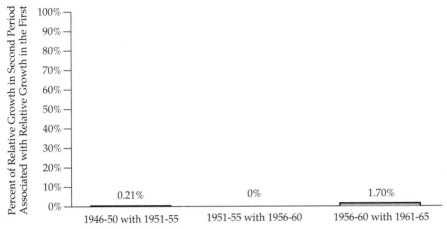

Source: Lintner, J. and R. Glauber, "Higgledy Piggledy Growth in America," (Unpublished paper presented to the Seminar on the Analysis of Security Prices, May 1967), University of Chicago, Table 3, Part (e).

FIGURE 4.3. Percentage of differential earnings growth in one 5-year period associated with earnings growth in the next period

one five-year period (1961–65) can be associated with growth differences in the preceding period.

If you're trying to forecast which stocks are going to grow the fastest in the next five years, you can forget about using the last five years as a guide. The past is *not* a very good guide to the future.

But extrapolation of past trend is at least the starting point, if not the basis, of most professional forecasts of earnings per share.

FLIP FOR IT

So firms aren't very consistent when it comes to their growth rankings *per se*. Are they at least consistent when it comes to rougher measures of relative performance, such as being better or worse than average from year to year?

Another British professor named Richard Brealey tried to find out.[11] He first ranks U.S. firms on the basis of their rate of growth in earnings per

[11]Brealey, R. A., *An Introduction to Risk and Return From Common Stocks*, (Cambridge, MA: MIT Press, 1969).

share. Then he notes whether a particular firm is in the top or bottom half of the rankings from year to year.

Suppose, for a given firm over a period of years, we observe the following sequence of top halves (+) and bottom halves (−):

$$+ \quad + \quad - \quad + \quad - \quad - \quad + \quad - \quad + \quad + \quad + \quad + \quad - \quad + \quad - \quad - \quad -$$

Brealey now tabulates the number of runs he sees of various lengths. For example, for how many years do we see the firm staying on the top or bottom for a *single* year before switching to the opposite position?

$$+ \quad + \quad \boxed{-} \; \boxed{+} \quad - \quad - \quad \boxed{+} \boxed{-} \quad + \quad + \quad + \quad + \quad \boxed{-} \boxed{+} \quad - \quad - \quad -$$

Three + runs of length 1 and three −.

Now how many runs of length 2?

$$\boxed{+ \quad +} \quad - \quad + \quad \boxed{- \quad -} \quad + \quad - \quad + \quad + \quad + \quad + \quad - \quad + \quad - \quad - \quad -$$

One + and one −.

$$+ \quad + \quad - \quad + \quad - \quad - \quad + \quad - \quad \boxed{+ \quad + \quad + \quad +} \quad - \quad + \quad \boxed{- \quad - \quad -}$$

And of length 3 and 4?

One − of length 3, and one + of length 4.

Brealey now runs this type of tabulation over all the firms in his sample.

But what if being in the top half or bottom half was simply a matter of luck?

We'll still see runs.

Flip a coin. If you're lucky, it won't take long before you flip five heads in a row. If you're flipping a fair coin, that's just a matter of luck.

However, count the number of runs in the won/loss records for the Chicago Bulls and the Dallas Mavericks and you *won't* conclude that success in basketball is just a matter of luck.

But what role does luck play in "winning" in growth in earnings per share?

A graph of Brealey's tabulation is presented in Figures 4.4A and 4.4B. The length of run is plotted horizontally; the number of runs he sees is plotted vertically.

The broken curve shows the number of runs you'd expect to see if being above or below average in earnings growth were simply a matter of chance.

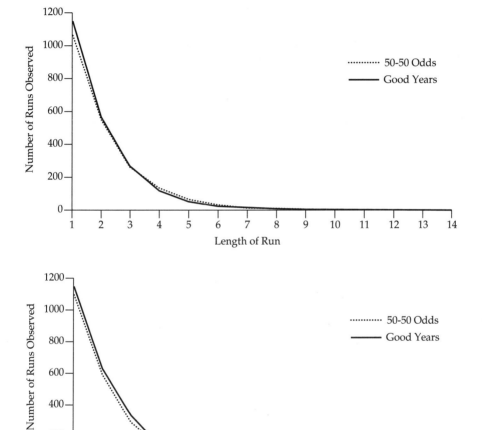

Source: Brealey, R., *An Introduction to Risk and Return from Common Stocks*, Second Edition. Cambridge, Mass.: 1983.

FIGURE 4.4. A. Actual number of runs of good years versus 50–50 odds. B. Actual number of runs of bad years versus 50–50 odds.

Simply a matter of flipping a coin.

Heads in the top half. Tails in the bottom.

The solid curves show the actual number of runs Brealey sees in his count.

Hard to tell the difference.

Note that we actually see more runs of short duration and fewer runs of long duration. This is consistent with short-run inertia and long-run reversal patterns in the growth of *earnings per share.*

Do you remember?

In Chapter 2 we found these types of patterns in *rates of return to stocks.*

We seem to have a degree of corroboration here.

So far, the "old timers" seem to have the upper hand.

THE CHRISTMAS TREE

Okay, so the past can't be counted on as a guide to the future. The stocks that grew the fastest in the past can't be counted on to repeat their relative performance in the future. If you're going to make a forecast of the future relative rate of growth in earnings, you had better be prepared to base your projection on something other than a simple extrapolation of *past trend.*

However, those who forecast the future *can* base their forecasts on a rich variety of information in addition to a firm's *past* growth behavior.

Relevant information might include valuable patent rights, market leadership, recognizable brand name, strategic location, and astute management. These and many more can help a firm carve out a position which is conducive to rapid growth in future earnings per share.

Given its access to this type of information, how accurate are the *market's forecasts* of relative rates of growth in earnings?

Unfortunately, the market's expectations are not published anywhere, so we can't directly check their accuracy. However, there are indicators that can be used as signals of what the market is thinking.

As we discussed in Chapter 1, the market price of a stock reflects the market's assessment of its future prospects. It's likely to be the case that, if the price is large relative to its accounting book value, the prospects are good. Conversely, a high book-to-price ratio would indicate that bad times are expected ahead.

The same is true for the relationship between market price and other accounting numbers such as earnings per share. If the price is large relative to current earnings, it is probably because the market is betting on *future* earnings being substantially larger than *current* earnings. Stocks with low ratios of earnings to price tend to be growth stocks; stocks with high ratios tend to be value stocks. But do growth stocks actually turn out to grow faster and value stocks slower than average? In the *future*. *After* they have been identified as growth or value by the market.

Three investment professionals named Fuller, Huberts, and Levinson (FHL) recently published an interesting study[12] which sheds a considerable amount of light on that question.

At the end of March in each year, during the period 1973 through 1990, FHL rank the firms in their study[13] by the ratio of the previous year's earnings per share to market price per share. (Presumably, by the end of March the previous year's earnings would have been announced by their firms.) The 20% of the firms with the largest ratio (value) go into the first group, the next 20% into the second group, down to the fifth group which contains the 20% with the lowest ratio (growth).[14] They then observe the relative rates of growth in earnings for each of the groups *in each of the next 8 years.*[15]

Do the value stocks actually turn out to grow more slowly than the growth stocks? If he were alive today, Benjamin Graham might be surprised to hear that the answer to that question is yes!

---

[12]Fuller, R.J., L.C. Huberts, and M.J. Levinson, "Returns to E/P Strategies; Higgledy Piggledy Growth; Analysts Forecast Errors; and Omitted Risk Factors," *The Journal of Portfolio Management*, Winter, 1993.

[13]To be included in their study a firm must have had a total market capitalization (price per share times total number of common shares outstanding) equal to at least 0.01% of the total value of the S&P 500 stock index. The number of stocks included in their study ranged from 887 in 1973 to 1179 in 1990.

[14]The groups are industry diversified, in that each group contains 20% of the firms in a particular industry.

[15]This process is repeated for as many years as their data would allow (from 1974 through 1992). Then the results are averaged across all the years.

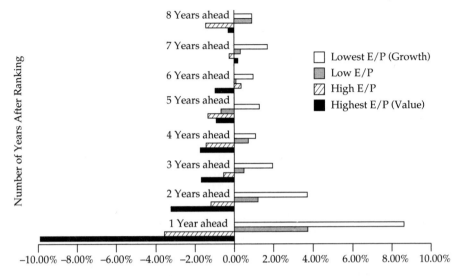

Growth in Earnings per Share Relative to Middle Quintile

Source: Fuller, R., L. Huberts, and M. Levinson, "Returns to E/P Strategies, Higgledy-Piggledy Growth, Analysts' Forecast Errors, and Omitted Risk Factors," *Journal of Portfolio Management*, Winter 1993, Exhibit 6.

FIGURE 4.5. **Relative subsequent growth in highest, high, low, and lowest quintiles of E/P ratio**

The results of the test are presented in Figure 4.5. Relative growth is plotted horizontally as the difference between growth of the groups with above or below average earnings-to-price ratios and the growth of the middle 20% of the firms. As we move up vertically, we move into the future relative to the year in which the stocks were ranked on the basis of their earnings-to-price ratios.

To illustrate, the firms with the highest ratios (value) grew nearly 10% slower (0.3% vs. 10.2%) than the middle group in the first year following the rankings. On the other hand, the firms with the lowest ratios (growth) grew nearly 9% faster (18.8% vs. 10.2%). It is also the case that the other, intermediate, groups fall right in line where you'd expect them to be.

This pattern persists in the second year following the ranking, and the third, and the fourth. The market, using whatever sources of information it uses, is clearly able to distinguish between the fast and slow growers for at least four years into the future.

Some have referred to this graph as "The Christmas Tree," based on the many presents I allege lie under its boughs. The Christmas Tree gives us the best look yet at the length of time separating the short run and the long run. It tells that profitability *tends* to revert to normal levels after a period of only a few years.

But how can we reconcile The Christmas Tree with the findings of L, RL, LG, and Brealey?

Keep in mind that most of the previous work was done by observing the growth behavior of individual firms, rather than large groups of stocks (like we're observing here). In addition the previous work was directed at the relationship between past and future growth, as opposed to the relationship between the *structure of current market prices* and future growth. In setting prices, the market can take into account many factors in addition to past growth.

The test of Figure 4.5 is still highly relevant because investors typically don't invest in *individual firms*. Rather, they invest (perhaps through mutual funds) in *large portfolios of many firms*, like the ones observed by FHL.

After seeing the results of their test, FHL conclude that (a) the results of earlier tests of "higgledy-piggledy growth" were mistaken and (b) that the superlative performance of value-oriented stocks recorded by many, including themselves, is not due to the tendency of the market to overreact to a firm's past growth record. However, as stated above, the earlier researchers were focusing on the relationship between the past and the future. FHL's results on the relationship between the levels of current stock prices and future growth don't show that the previous authors were mistaken about the missing link between the past and the future.

In addition, the issue is the *actual speed* of the reversion to the mean growth rate of the middle group, as evident in Figure 4.5, *relative to what was anticipated by the market* in setting the market prices for the stocks and the related ratios of earnings per share to market price.

The results of Figure 4.5 indicate that future growth pretty much reverts to the mean after five or six years. Was this what the market expected in setting the prices for the stocks in each group? *If you buy the growth stocks and their growth rates revert to the mean that quickly, what will the returns on your investment in growth stocks be relative to an investment in value stocks?*

• • •

"Your Honor."

"Yes, Professor Haugen."

"If the Court pleases, I would like to reserve the right to recall The Christmas Tree later in these proceedings."

"We can't afford to waste time repeating ourselves, Professor Haugen. Are you sure that a recall of The Christmas Tree will prove to be enlightening?"

"I am *quite* sure, Your Honor."

Chapter Five

THE RACE BETWEEN VALUE AND GROWTH

IN SEARCH OF MEDIOCRITY

Perhaps you have heard of the best seller, *In Search of Excellence: Lessons from America's Best Run Corporations.*[1] The authors of this book took a list of companies considered to be innovative by a group of informed businessmen, and screened them on the following six measures of long-run financial superiority:

1. Rate of growth in corporate assets (1961–80)
2. Rate of growth in book value (1961–80)
3. Average ratio of market price to book value (1961–80)
4. Average return on corporate assets[2] (1961–80)
5. Average return on book value (1962–80)
6. Average ratio of net income to sales (1961–80)

In studying the companies that passed the screen, the authors were able to identify the attributes that these companies seemed to have in common—the lessons.

In 1987, a money manager named Michelle Clayman published an article[3] in which she tracked the performance of the stocks of these companies in a period following the ranking, 1981 through 1985.

---

[1]Peters, T.J., and R.H. Waterman, *In Search of Excellence: Lessons from America's Best-run Corporations,* (New York: Harper and Row, 1982).
[2]Return on total assets was measured by net income divided by the aggregate of long-term debt, preferred stock, and book value of common equity.
[3]Clayman, M., "In Search of Excellence: The Investor's Viewpoint," *Financial Analysts' Journal,* May–June, 1987.

These firms had established strong records of performance prior to 1980. By 1980 they had become growth stocks. If the market overreacted and overpriced them, their performance after 1980 should be poor as the market corrects, and the prices of the stocks fall to more reasonable levels.

Clayman compares the performance of the "excellent" companies with another group which she calls "unexcellent." These were the 39 companies in the S&P 500 population that had the worst combination of the 6 characteristics as of the end of 1980 (value stocks).

A comparison of the excellent and the unexcellent, in terms of the 6 characteristics, can be seen in Figure 5.1. As you can see, the bad are truly bad. Slow rates of growth. Low market to book. And suffering in income available to stockholders.

But Clayman reveals that the stunning characteristics of the excellent companies quickly reverted toward the mean in the years that followed their

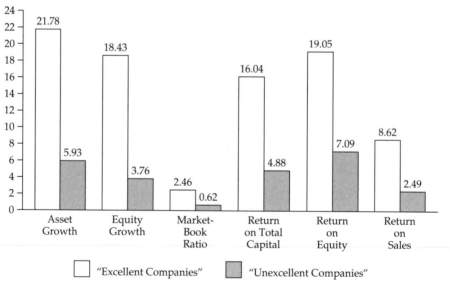

Source: Clayman, M., "In Search of Excellence: The Investor's Viewpoint," *Financial Analysts' Journal*, May–June 1987, Figure B, p. 58.

FIGURE 5.1. Characteristics of "excellent" and "unexcellent" companies (1976–1980)

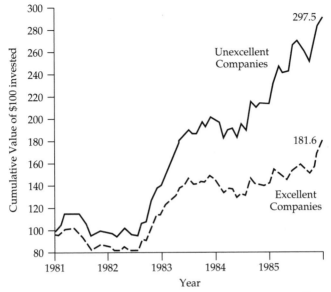

Source: Clayman, M., "In Search of Excellence: The Investor's Viewpoint, *Financial Analysts' Journal,* May–June 1987, p. 63.

FIGURE 5.2. "Excellent and unexcellent" cumulative return, 1981–85

1980 screening. Rates of growth in assets and book value nearly halved. Significant reductions were experienced in the other 4 categories as well.

As I. M. D. Little and others discovered, it is difficult to remain outstanding in a competitive world for very long.

The unexcellent companies also reverted toward the mean. They showed substantial improvement in their median values for all 6 categories. Once again, the market didn't anticipate the mean reversion.

The relative performance of the two groups of companies is presented in Figure 5.2.

Value wins.

The book *In Search of Excellence* may well be quite valuable to the prospective managers of innovative firms, but the successful investor should look more favorably on those firms which have been the mirror images *in the past* of those touted in the book.

THE MANY FACES OF VALUE AND GROWTH

The ratio of book to market may be an important clue for those seeking to find value stocks and avoid growth stocks, but it is not the only one.

A large pension consulting firm, DeMarche Associates, has created and tracked the performance history of a large array of stylized stock indexes. The weights assigned to the individual stocks in the indexes are similar to those in the S&P 500—they are proportional to the sizes of the individual companies.[4] However, each of the DeMarche indexes contains stocks that are distinctive in some respect. For example, one index always contains the 25% of stocks with the highest ratio of price to earnings per share.

Armed with their array of indexes, DeMarche can track the relative performances of stocks with different characteristics.

And we can use the indexes to track the long-term performances of stocks with growth and value characteristics. Based on their gleaming *future* prospects, growth stocks have high prices in relation to their current levels of earnings per share and dividends per share. The market expects growth stocks to grow at a faster than average rate in the future. This expectation is likely to be based on the fact that growth has been substantially faster than average in the past. Thus, growth stocks should also be characterized by faster than average growth in past earnings.

The opposite is true for value stocks. Low prices are relative to current income and dividend levels. Slower than average trailing growth.

So to track the relative performance of growth and value, we shall select the following pairs of DeMarche indexes:[5]

1. The index containing the 25% of the stocks with the highest ratio of market price to current earnings per share[6] (growth) and the 25% with the lowest (value).

---

[4]Actually the weights are based on the total market capitalization of each stock—market price per share times the number of shares outstanding.

[5]All the DeMarche indexes considered here are constructed from the largest 1,600 U.S. stocks.

[6]In forming the index, DeMarche uses the most recently reported earnings per share as of the date the index is constructed. This is also true of the other indexes considered here.

2. The index containing the 25% of the stocks with the lowest ratio of dividends per share to market price (growth) and the 25% with the highest (value).

3. The index containing the 25% of the stocks with the fastest trailing growth rates in earnings per share (growth) and the 25% with the slowest (value).[7]

The cumulative value of a dollar invested in each of the six indexes (January 1968 through May 1993) is presented in Figure 5.3. The dark line in the middle shows the result of investing a dollar in the S&P 500.

Value wins again with all three means of separating growth from value. The value indexes outperform the S&P, while growth underperforms.

When you try to reach for GO, you will probably be dealing with mutual funds. These funds will probably not advertise themselves as GO

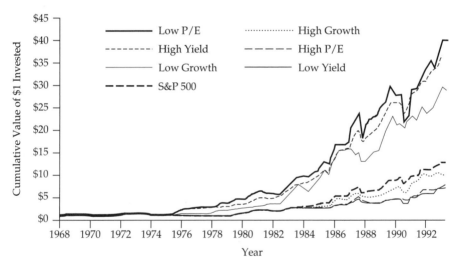

Source: DeMarche Associates.

FIGURE 5.3. Cumulative value of $1 invested in various forms of value and growth

[7]DeMarche actually splits stocks into four groups on the basis of trailing growth: (a) better than a 10% rate over the preceding 6 to 10 years; (b) between 6% and 10%; (c) less than 6%; and finally a variable growth group which has shown combined declines in earnings over any two years which exceeded the average growth rate for the 6–10-year period.

investors. To find out if they travel the route to Diamond Head, you will have to determine if they are truly value-oriented investors.

Based on what we saw in Chapter 1, a high, overall ratio of book to price for their portfolio would be a positive sign.

However, the managers of many mutual funds don't keep track of the book-to-price ratio for their portfolios. They are more likely to know the average dividend-to-price ratio or the earnings-to-price ratios.

Based on what we've seen here, these are also trusty beacons which light your way. Book-to-market value may be good, but it's not that special.

Now an important aside.

Note that the path of the S&P 500 is closer to the growth indexes than to the value. This is because, as we shall clearly see below, *growth stocks tend to be large companies.* Value stocks tend to be small companies. Since there is an equal number of stocks in each index within a pair, the growth index will constitute a larger fraction of the S&P than the value.

This means that the S&P 500 stock index is heavily invested in growth stocks. Interesting!

Many pension funds and other institutional investors like to invest large chunks of their money in portfolios that replicate the composition of the S&P. They call this strategy *indexing.*

Based on what we are seeing, indexing doesn't seem to be a very smart move on their part.

These results show that GO is clearly a valuable strategy in the long term, but how reliable is it in the short term? After all, if it doesn't work for a while, some of us may panic and give up.

Fortunately for the impatient, it's pretty reliable.

In Figure 5.4 we show the rolling difference in the performance of two portfolios (value and growth). The value portfolio is equally invested in the low price-to-earnings index, the high dividend-to-price index, and the slow trailing growth index. The growth portfolio is equally invested in the three growth counterparts.

Starting in 1968, we observe the rolling difference between average 5-year returns to the value of growth composite. Note that in 1973, the end of the first 5-year period, growth has slightly beaten value over the previous 5

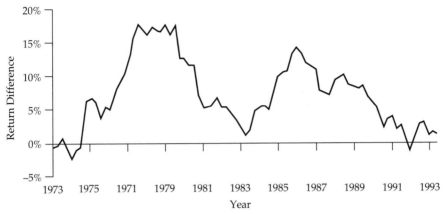

FIGURE 5.4. Rolling annualized average 5-year difference between the returns to value and growth composites

years. As we move on, however, value takes on and maintains the upper hand until the period ending in 1992.

Even if you're prone to panic, if you can hold out for 5 years, you're highly likely to see GO smile upon you.

REMOVING THE SIZE EFFECT FROM GO

Irrespective of their growth or value characteristics, small stocks tend to produce greater than average rates of return.

This may be because investors consider them to be (a) riskier or (b) more costly to trade. Information about the nature and activities of small stocks is more scarce. They are also less actively traded, so dealers may establish a larger spread between the price they are willing to buy and the price they are willing to sell, so they can make a decent "buck" while making a market for the stocks.

For whatever reason, for long periods of time (at least since 1926), they have tended to produce higher rates of return.

We now know that value stocks *tend* to be small stocks. This means that *a part* of GO is not the result of market overreaction, but rather, simply the result of investing in the more profitable small stocks.

How much?

Three professors named Lakonishok, Shleifer, and Vishny (LSV) attempted to find out.[8]

LSV also rank stocks by book/market.[9] They then form portfolios. The 10% of the stocks with the largest ratio of book to market go into portfolio #1, the next 10% into portfolio #2, and so on. The portfolios are re-formed annually, and their performance is observed over the next five years. This process begins in 1968–72 and continues through the final five-year period, 1985–89.

LSV adjust the returns for size by subtracting from the monthly return of each stock the monthly return from a portfolio of comparable size. In an overreactive market, value stocks should outperform other stocks in their size class, and growth stocks should underperform.

We see that this is indeed the case in Figure 5.5, where we plot the average annual over- or underperformance across all of their 5-year periods. In

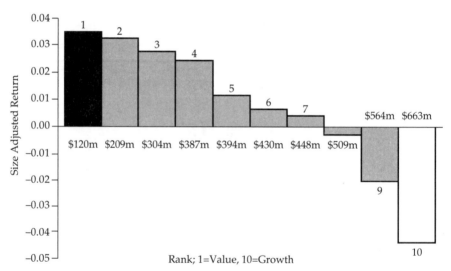

Source: Lakonishok, J., A. Schleifer, and R. Vishny, "Contrarian Investment, Extrapolation, and Risk," Working Paper 93-0128, University of Illinois at Urbana-Champaign.

FIGURE 5.5. Size-adjusted returns to value and growth

---

[8]Lakonishok, J., A. Schleifer, and R. Vishny, "Contrarian Investment, Extrapolation and Risk," working paper, Bureau of Economic and Business Research, University of Illinois at Urbana-Champaign.

[9]The rankings are made in April of each year based on book value for the previous year. The individual stocks in each portfolio are then assumed to be bought and held for one year. At the end of the year the stocks are reranked on the basis of book to market value and the portfolios are re-formed.

the extreme groupings, value is outperforming by about 3.5% and growth underperforming by more than 4%.

Note that, once again, performance falls steadily and reliably as we move from value to growth.

The average size (market price per share times number of shares) is also listed in the Figure, so you can see that growth stocks really are larger companies.

GO-ING AROUND THE WORLD

Human behavior is human behavior, wherever we live. Moreover, while it has lost its position at the head of the pack in many areas, *the U.S. is still the world's leader in finance.* If we embrace things like growth stocks, the rest of the world will also. Overreacting is catchy.

Carlo Capaul, Ian Rowley, and Nobel laureate (for CAPM) William Sharpe (CRS) recently published a study[10] to determine whether value also outperforms growth abroad.

CRS create value and growth stock indexes for various countries. They start with the population of stocks in a country's major index (such as the S&P 500 for the U.S.).[11]

For the S&P they rank the 500 stocks, at a given point of time, by the ratio of a firm's most recently available book-to-market number. They then go down the list from highest toward lowest until they reach the half-way point, where the total market value (price times number of shares) of all the stocks in the top half is approximately equal to the total market value of the bottom half. The top becomes the value index, the bottom the growth. The indexes are re-formed at six-month intervals. They then observe the relative returns to the value and growth indexes from January 1981 through June 1992.

The average annualized difference between the returns to value and growth is plotted in Figure 5.6.

Value wins once again. In every country observed.

---

[10]Capaul, C., I. Rowley, and W. Sharpe, "International Value and Growth Stock Returns," *Financial Analysts' Journal*, January–February, 1993.
[11]The indexes used are those published by Morgan Stanley Capital International.

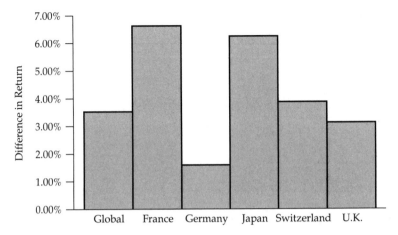

Source: Capaul, C., I. Rowley, and W. Sharpe, "International Value and Growth Stock Returns," *Financial Analysts Journal,* Jan.–Feb. 1993, Table IV, p. 34.

FIGURE 5.6. **The spread in annualized returns between value and growth**

The global number reflects a composite of the five foreign countries plus the U.S. (Yes, they verified the value return premium in the U.S. as well.)

By now it should be evident that what we have seen in the United States data is not a fluke, but rather a phenomenon of fundamental importance that we should be concerned about, if it stems from risk, or that we should be prepared to take advantage of, if it stems from overreaction.

THE DEBATE OVER THE NATURE OF GO

Even the Zealots who still cling tenaciously to the tenets of market efficiency believe that The Theory (CAPM) must go.

They have seen and have verified that the Golden Opportunity exists. Many others[12] had reported of the existence of GO decades before, but the

[12] See for example Basu, S., "The Investment Performance of Common Stocks in Relation to their Price-Earnings Ratios," *The Journal of Finance,* June, 1977; Basu, S., "The Relationship Between Earnings Yield, Market Value and Return for NYSE Common Stocks," *The Journal of Financial Economics,* June, 1983; Breen, W., "Low Price-Earnings Ratios and Industry Relatives," *Financial Analysts' Journal,* July–August, 1968; Huang, S., "Study of the Performance of Rapid Growth Stocks," *Financial Analysts Journal,* January–February, 1965; Flugel, F.K., "The Rate of Return on High and Low P/E Ratio Stocks," *Financial Analysts Journal,* November–December, 1968.

Zealots scoffed because they believed the methods used to measure the performance of value strategies were flawed.

The reason the Fama-French study of Chapter 1 made headlines was that Fama, *a long-time champion of CAPM (The Theory) and market efficiency (The Fantasy),* was one of the authors.

The Pope said God was dead.

At least the God of CAPM.

The God of *The Fantasy* was, apparently, very much alive.

But how to explain GO? How to explain the premium to value investing?

Aha! What we've got here is a *risk* premium.

It's *not* the artifact of corrected overreaction. It's *not* a surprise.

You see the Zealots believe that everyone knows, and has known, about GO all along. Everyone knows you can get to Diamond Head by investing in value stocks. However we're not all packing our bags because it seems that the trip doesn't have much appeal.

Let The Fantasy speak:

"It seems that value stocks have low current prices and high future returns because they are *risky.*"

According to the latest versions of The Fantasy, value stocks are "Fallen Angels." The stocks of once successful companies whose fortunes have long since turned against them. They've been so beaten up that they now *scare the daylights out of us.*[13]

In fact, they scare us so much that many of us refuse to invest in them even though we believe that doing so will ultimately take us all the way to

---

[13]In Lakonishok, J., A. Shleifer, and R. Vishny, "Contrarian Investment, Extrapolation and Risk," working paper. Bureau of Economic and Business Research, University of Illinois at Urbana-Champaign, value stocks are found to outperform the market index on average over the index's worst 25 months of performance, over the best 25 months of performance, over the negative performance months, and over the positive performance months. (See their Table 7.)

Diamond Head. Many people are so scared that they willingly shun Diamond Head (retiring at roughly $280,000 per year) and set their sights on Diamond Bar (roughly $2,700 per year) instead.

Yes, *knowingly* and *willingly* pick Diamond *Bar*. So says The Fantasy.

The Fallen Angels must be scary indeed!

But wait a minute. Remember Figure 1.3? According to F&F themselves, value stocks have lower risk.

So what's to be scared about?

Whatever's supposed to be scaring us isn't showing up in instability of the prices of value stocks.

Most of the time, stock prices change because of the arrival of new information.

What's scaring us won't show up in price instability if we don't periodically hear new things about it.

There's a monster sleeping under your bed. It scares the living daylights out of you, but it's sleeping. Your bedroom is, and has been, very quiet. Makes no difference. You're still scared.

Value stocks might be plagued by *sleeping monsters*.

An example of a sleeping monster?

Hard to find, but I can think of at least one.

Think about a nice, stable, unexciting public utility stock. Risky? Doesn't appear to be based on the behavior of its stock price. But is there something quietly underlying the situation that terrifies investors anyway?

Possibly.

What about the possibility of a major change in technology. A change in the way we communicate over long distances. A change in the way we generate power. A change that would render the franchise of the utility *obsolete*. Overnight. A change that would cause the market price of the utility's stock to plummet. A lurking source of investor terror. But the utility's stock price is stable nevertheless because we don't get new information which periodically raises or lowers the probability that this monster will awaken and proceed to gobble utility investors up.

The problem with this story is that we need many different breeds of monsters because there are many different kinds of value stocks breeding in many different types of industries.

And it's hard to come up with new monster stories.

Moreover, it's been shown that GO is an intraindustry effect and not an interindustry effect.[14] We, apparently, don't see a value premium in going from one industry to the next.

That means that it's going to be even tougher to come up with new and exciting sleeping monster stories. They can't be like the utility story. That's an *industry story*. Stories like that are consistent with GO premiums across different industries, and we just don't see them.

Believers in The Fantasy have a really tough job ahead of them.

And what about the growth stocks? The Fantasy says that we know that they will have low returns, we know that they will take us to Diamond *Bar*. We go anyway because we are allegedly so *fond of the ride*.

But why aren't we afraid of the many bumps along the way? Why aren't we concerned about the volatility that we see in them in Figure 1.3? What's going to save us? Who will ultimately show up to rescue us from the wild swings in our performance to make us confident that we will eventually end up at Diamond *Bar*?

Silent Angels?

---

[14]See Kothari, S.P., J. Shanken, and R.G. Sloan, "Another Look at the Cross-section of Stock Returns," Bradley Policy Research Center Working Paper, William E. Simon Graduate School of Business, University of Rochester. In their paper they find that GO tends to disappear when cap-weighted industry indexes are ranked, rather than individual firms. The authors contend that the industry indexes suffer less from survival bias problems. However, the clear presence of GO in studies commencing after 1980 as well as its presence in studies presented in the next chapter which are cleaned of survival bias, indicates that its disappearance in an industry study is due to something else. Many industries are dominated by one or two relatively large firms. *To the extent that GO is a minor factor for the largest firms, it is likely to disappear when cap-weighted industry indexes are used to find it.* Moreover, differences in book to price from one industry to the next are more likely to be related to the relative amount of capital employed in production functions than to overreaction.

WHEN WE GO TO DIAMOND HEAD

There is another problem with The Fantasy's risk premium story.

If GO really represents the delivery of a risk premium, it should be earned uniformly through time. At least with the same uniformity that investors are *exposed* and *sensitized* to risk.[15]

However, we learned from Figure 2.4A and 2.4B that a *big* chunk of GO comes at the 3-day window of time *when firms announce their earnings.* We Heretics claim that the market is being caught by surprise—growth stocks reporting unexpectedly bad earnings and value unexpectedly good.

Believers in The Fantasy must argue that risk is especially high during these periods, and that the relatively high returns to value are risk premiums being earned as the risk is experienced. *But the Zealots must come up with believable explanations for the following observations* for the earnings announcement dates:

(a) Why does the relative uncertainty in general go *up* for the value stocks (they generally produce high returns around earnings announcements) and *down* for the growth stocks (their returns are low)?

(b) Why does the relative risk switch around (as we see in Figure 2.4a and 2.4b) after the 8th month following rankings of performance over the previous 6 months? We have argued that the inefficient market fails to recognize a good report as a precursor of a few more to follow. When they come, it overreacts, thinking the string will continue unabated for a long period into the future. But how can the Zealots explain the switch in terms of shifts in *relative* risk?

And here's a result that should prove even more puzzling to believers in The Fantasy.

Three more professors named Chopra, Lakonishok, and Ritter (CLR) find that the rest of GO comes at *the turn of the year.*[16]

---

[15]Not only is it possible that the level of risk changes over time, but it is also possible that changes in the level of risk aversion change as we go through different points in the business cycle where investors earn different levels of income.

[16]Chopra, N., J. Lakonishok, and J. Ritter, "Measuring Abnormal Performance: Do stocks overreact?," *Journal of Financial Economics,* April, 1992, p. 235.

CLR rank the stocks in their study on the basis of the return over the previous 5 years.[17] They put the 5% of the stocks with the worst trailing 5-year records into group #1, the 5% with the second worst into group #2, and so on through group #20, the growth stocks.

The average monthly return to these stocks during the 5 years *after they are ranked* is plotted in Figure 5.7. The monthly average returns in January are shown in the rear, and the average returns for the other months are shown in the front.[18]

Incredible!

The value stocks produce *huge* January returns, relative to the growth stocks.[19]

Why?

This is not an especially risky period for the value stocks. Nor is it an especially safe one for the growth stocks.

It is, however, an especially active period for many money managers.

Managers who have done well during the year have an incentive to lock-in their performance as they approach the winter months. Bonuses don't increase much when great performance becomes really great, but they shrink dramatically if great becomes mediocre.

So if you've got great performance, lock in. How? Your performance is probably measured relative to the S&P 500 index. As you liquidate your profitable aggressive positions, park the proceeds in blue-chip stocks that behave like your benchmark.

---

[17]CLR look at New York stock exchange firms over the period 1926 through 1986. The results of Figure 5.7 reflect averages of five-year windows of time over this entire period.

[18]CLR also find that a large chunk of GO comes in three-day windows around earnings announcement days. Their results are similar to those of Jegadeesh and Titman (Figures 2.4A and 2.4B), except that CLR initially rank stocks on the basis of their total returns over the past *five years* rather than the *6-month* period used by JT. Because they rank on the basis of the longer period, they find evidence of the long-term reversal pattern, but they fail to detect the short-term inertia pattern in returns.

[19]This result was discovered first by DeBondt, W., and R. Thaler, "Does the Stock Market Overreact?" *Journal of Finance*, July, 1985.

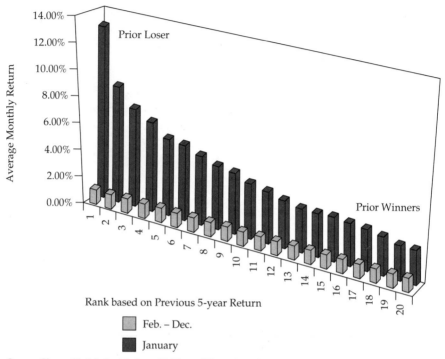

Source: Chopra N., J. Lakonishok, and J. Ritter, "Measuring Abnormal Performance: Do Stocks Overreact?" *Journal of Financial Economics*, April 1992, Vol. 31, No. 2, Table 3.

FIGURE 5.7. Seasonal returns to value and growth portfolios

Same thing if you're doing really badly. Lock-out disaster by selling off the sour notes. Replace them with blue chips that will look good to your clients when they inspect the portfolio at the end of the year. By investing in blue-chip stocks, which comprise a big part of your benchmark for the remainder of the year, you keep your relative performance out of the disaster zone.

The process of locking in good performance and locking out disaster takes place at different times for different managers during the later part of the year.

Going back, however, is a different story.

On the morning of the first trading day of the year, the starter's gun is raised into the air and fired.

The race to beat the market is on for a fresh calendar year.

The pros who locked in or locked out simultaneously move back.

But they move back selectively, looking to buy the stocks they believe are undervalued. Looking for bargains. Stocks that have been driven down too far. Looking to avoid or sell short stocks that are overvalued. Stocks selling at bloated prices.

Because the pros all move at once, their trades bump stock prices, pushing the bargains up and the bloated down.

What we're seeing in Figure 5.7 is not the delivery of a risk premium. There is nothing especially risky about the month of January. Instead, we're seeing the tracks of stocks being pushed back to equilibrium levels.

Stocks that had been over- or undervalued by an overreactive market.

GO is *not* a risk premium expected by a rational and efficient market.

It is a surprise.[20]

---

[20]In a recent paper (Fama, E.F. and K.R. French, "Common Risk Factors in the Returns on Stocks and Bonds," *Journal of Financial Economics*, February, 1993, pp. 3–56) F&F show (their Table 9a, Panel iv.) that in market environments where (a) the performance of high and low book/price stocks are equal, (b) the performance of large and small stocks are equal, and (c) the broad market index produces a return equal to the risk-free rate, we should not expect to see any of the size or book/price based quintiles outperforming. This, of course, is not very convincing to the Heretics. They want proof that the road to Diamond Head is fraught with perils. They also want to know why the premium to value is delivered with such a peculiar seasonal pattern—a pattern that fits nicely with the overreactive market hypothesis. *It is not sufficient to merely call the premium to value investing a risk premium.*

Chapter Six

"V"

ONE-MONTH HORIZON TEST OF THE RELATIONSHIP BETWEEN RISK AND EXPECTED RETURN

Let's re-cap some of the things we've learned so far:

(a) Value stocks tend to produce higher returns; growth stocks tend to produce lower returns.

(b) Value stocks tend to be less risky; growth stocks tend to be more risky.

Given (a) and (b), it would seem that we can deduce:

(c) *Low-risk stocks have high expected returns; high-risk stocks have low expected returns.*

But a typical MBA will tell you: "In the stock market, risk and return are *positively* related—the greater the risk, the greater the expected return."

That's because the MBA was carefully trained to believe in both The Theory and The Fantasy.

Although Fama and French do not *admit* that (c) above is evident in their results, a closer look reveals that it is.

In Figures 6.1 through 6.10 we plot the relationship between risk (beta) and realized return for the ten size groupings (6.1 the smallest stocks, 6.10

the largest) analyzed by Fama and French.[1] We have drawn standard regression lines[2] through each of the scatter plots. *All of the lines have negative slopes*, although all are not significantly negative.

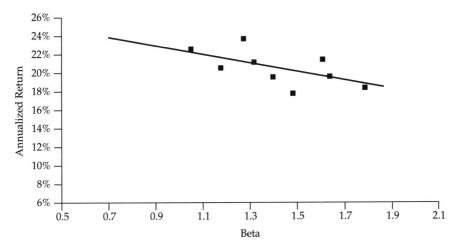

FIGURE 6.1. A test of the risk-return relationship using one-month horizon: decile 1: smallest stocks (1963–1990) (two deciles overlap)

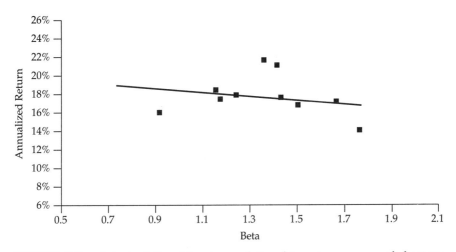

FIGURE 6.2. A test of the risk-return relationship using one-month horizon: decile 2 (1963–1990)

[1]The graphs are taken from Table I, Panels A and B of Fama, E. and K. French, "The Cross-Section of Expected Stock Returns." *The Journal of Finance,* June, 1992, pp. 427–466.
[2]Lines that will minimize the sum of the squared vertical distances from the line.

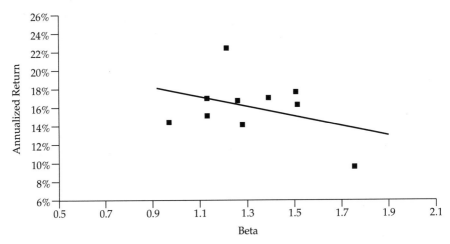

FIGURE 6.3. A test of the risk-return relationship using one-month horizon: decile 3 (1963–1990)

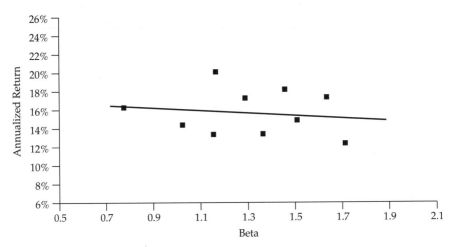

FIGURE 6.4. A test of the risk-return relationship using one-month horizon: decile 4 (1963–1990)

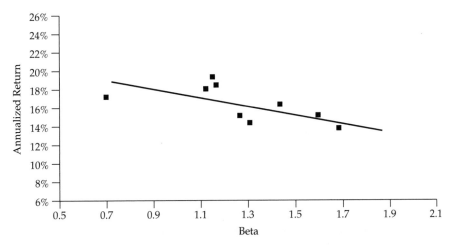

FIGURE 6.5. A test of the risk-return relationship using one-month horizon: decile 5 (1963–1990) (two deciles overlap)

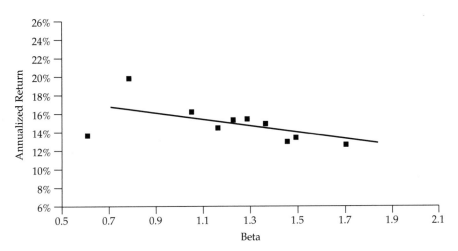

FIGURE 6.6. A test of the risk-return relationship using one-month horizon: decile 6 (1963–1990)

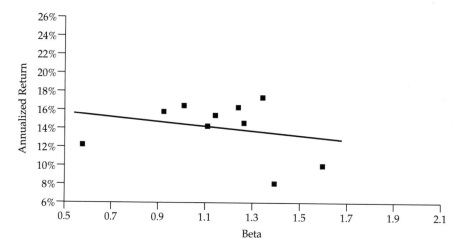

FIGURE 6.7. A test of the risk-return relationship using one-month horizon: decile 7 (1963–1990)

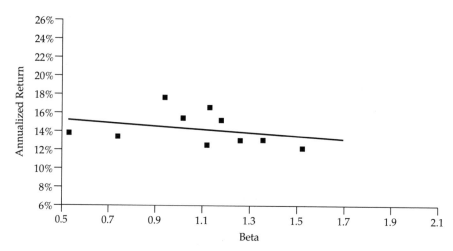

FIGURE 6.8. A test of the risk-return relationship using one-month horizon: decile 8 (1963–1990)

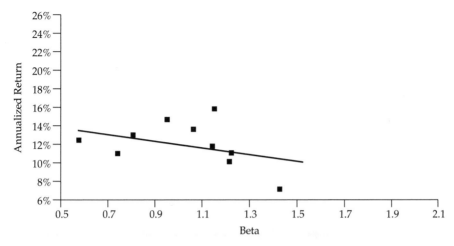

FIGURE 6.9. A test of the risk-return relationship using one-month horizon: decile 9 (1963–1990)

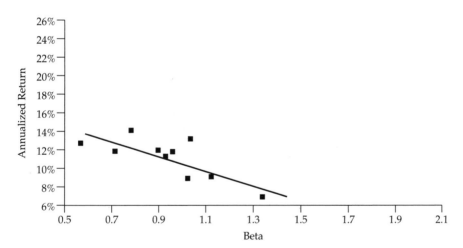

Source: Fama, E., and K. French, "The Cross-Section of Expected Stock Returns," *Journal of Finance,* June 1992, Table I.

FIGURE 6.10. A test of the risk-return relationship using one-month horizon: decile 10: largest stocks (1963–1990)

We suspect, however, that more would have been significant had a proper measure of return been plotted on the vertical scales.

THE NEGLECTED HORIZON PROBLEM

Fama and French observe the relationship between risk and the simple average of the monthly rates of return to their stock portfolios. This procedure is unbiased if the horizon of investors is of 1-month duration. *If the horizon of investors is longer than this, however, the slope estimates of Fama and French are upward biased.*

To see this, suppose that the investment horizon is in fact five years. To keep things simple, suppose also that investors expect the same realized return on all stocks and stock portfolios over this 5-year horizon. The realized return will be the geometric mean[3] of the monthly returns produced over the period.

We know that, if volatility is non-zero, the simple average is always greater than the geometric mean, and the difference increases proportionately with the volatility.

Consider the following example. Two portfolios and two periods. Both portfolios are worth $100 at the beginning of the first and at the end of the second period. However, in the interim Portfolio 1 falls to $50 and Portfolio 2 falls to $25. What is the simple average of their one-period returns? For Portfolio 1 it is 25% ({−50% + 100%}/2). For Portfolio 2, the more volatile, it is 112.5% ({−75% + 300%}/2).

The numbers 25% and 112.5% are unbiased estimates if the true horizon is one period long. However, they are upward biased if the true horizon is two periods, and the bias is greater for the more volatile portfolio.

Thus, if the true horizon is something like five years, and we assume instead that it is a month, we will find a positive relationship between volatility (and most likely beta) and the mean of monthly returns, even if there is no relationship between portfolio volatility and the true expected return over five years.

To see the extent of the bias, we'll perform the following experiment:

---

[3]The geometric mean is the nth root of the product of one plus each of the n monthly returns earned over the horizon period. It will be the investor's realized return if interim returns are reinvested in the portfolio.

Assume that investors have a *5-year horizon*. Also assume that they don't care about risk, so over the 5-year period all stocks have the same expected rate of return. Now pull, at random, 20 5-year "portfolio" returns from a probability distribution with a 15% annual expected return and a 20% annual volatility. Next compute the arithmetic mean of the 20 annualized 5-year returns as well as their actual volatility. Plot this first portfolio as one of the points in Figure 6.11.

Now repeat the process 199 times for 200 portfolios in all, each having a 15% expected annual return but a different volatility,[4] and plot each simulated portfolio as a point in Figure 6.11.

Note that there is no significant relationship between risk and realized 5-year return.[5]

Okay, now back to the first portfolio of the 200. This time take a distribution of monthly returns that corresponds to the annual return distribution with the 15% expected annualized return and the 20% annualized

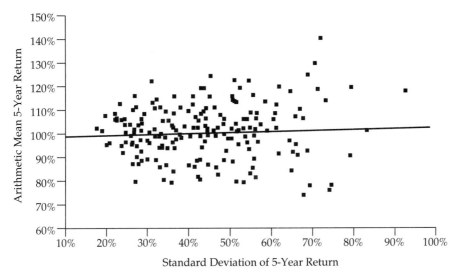

FIGURE 6.11. 5-Year arithmetic mean return versus 5-year standard deviation for 200 stocks with equal 5-year expected returns but differential standard deviations

[4]Ranging from 10% to 30% annualized.
[5]The coefficient of determination is .92% and the T-value for the slope is 1.35.

volatility. Pull 60 returns from the distribution, representing the 60 months in the first 5-year period. Scale these returns so that they compound to the first 5-year return pulled for the first portfolio. Repeat the same process for the other 19 returns pulled for the portfolio. You now have a series of 1,200 monthly rates of return that are consistent with the sequence of 20 5-year returns. Plot the mean of the 5-year returns against the volatility of the monthly returns as one of the points in Figure 6.12.

Next repeat the process 199 times and plot the 200 portfolios in Figure 6.12.

Note that there is no significant relationship between risk and return.[6]

Now we'll do what nearly everyone has done.

This time we'll compute the mean of the 1,200 monthly rates of return for each portfolio and plot them against their monthly volatilities in Figure 6.13.

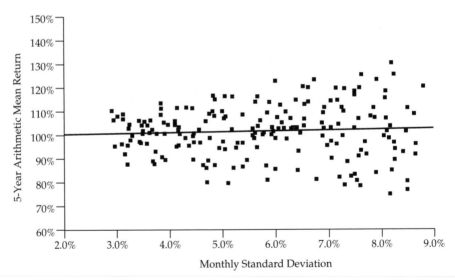

FIGURE 6.12. 5-Year arithmetic mean return versus 5-year monthly standard deviation for 200 stocks with equal 5-year expected returns but differential standard deviations

[6]The coefficient of determination is .32%, and the T-value for the slope is .79.

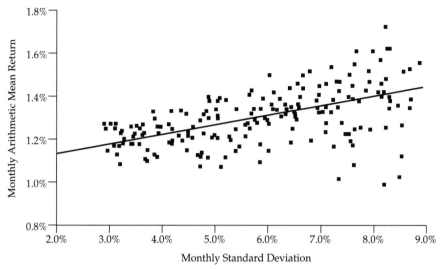

FIGURE 6.13. Monthly arithmetic mean return versus monthly standard deviation for 200 stocks with equal 5-year expected returns but differential standard deviations

Aha!

We find a positive relationship.

And it's highly significant, with a coefficient of determination of 28.94% and a T-value for the slope of 8.98.

That's one of the best results for the cross-section of risk and return ever found!

And we found it in a market where investors don't care about risk.

There are no risk premiums in our assumed market. But we find what looks like evidence supporting the existence of risk premiums if we assume that the investment horizon is shorter than it truly is.

F&F provide no support for their assumed 1-month horizon period. We don't really know the length of the true horizon, but I would find it easier to support the assumption of 5 years over 1 month. Quarters, as opposed to months, are the basic unit for measuring returns in the investment business. Five years is the typical interval for reconsideration of major asset allocation decisions by many pension funds. Five years is also an important period for the analysis of the performance of investment managers. Most funds will not tolerate underperformance across a full 5-year period. Moreover, 5 years span a typical cycle in business conditions.

We will examine the relationship between risk and return using a 5-year investment horizon later in this chapter. For now, we turn to another issue that has been raised regarding the FF results. Since FF re-rank and re-form their portfolios annually, there is considerable turnover within the portfolios. Moreover, F&F assume that the portfolios are weighted equally at the beginning of each month. There is nothing wrong with this, given an objective to investigate the properties of the cross-section of stock returns. However, a more practical question remains: "Can we really expect portfolios of low-volatility stocks to outperform their high-volatility counterparts in actual practice?" To answer this question, we must turn to simulations which impose realistic constraints on portfolio positions and portfolio turnover.

THEORY: WEST BY SOUTHWEST; EAST BY NORTHEAST

Question: "If we attempt to build low-volatility portfolios, what happens to our performance?"

CAPM predicts that the most comprehensive stock market indexes carry the highest possible expected returns, given their risk exposures. They are supposed to be positioned on, or very close to, the curve depicted in Figure 6.14.

Harry Markowitz's efficient set—the portfolios (or combinations of stocks) with the highest possible expected returns for their risk exposures.

Consistent with The Theory's prediction, the big dot in the figure is supposed to represent a major stock market index like the S&P 500.

As in Chapter 3, the little circles in the figure represent individual common stocks. In The Theory, there is supposed to be a rough, positive slope to the scatter of the positions of individual stocks in diagrams like these—the high-risk stocks falling in the northeast and the low-risk stocks falling in the southwest.

Suppose this were actually true.

What would we expect to happen if we tried to build a stock portfolio with the lowest risk in terms of periodic volatility of return?

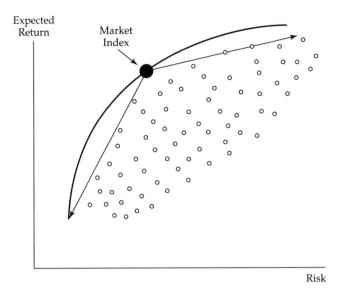

FIGURE 6.14. Effects of raising or lowering risk according to The Theory

Mind you, we're not trying to go for higher, or even lower, expected return. We're just trying to move as far *west* as possible in terms of the diagram.

Harry's Tool will help us find the right combination of stocks that will give us the lowest potential for future volatility of return.

In the context of Figure 6.14 and The Theory, a deliberate attempt to go west should be accompanied by a move to the *south.*

This is because we are aiming for the nose of the bullet (the lowest-risk portfolio), and The Theory predicts that the nose lies to the southwest of the market index.

Attempt to go west, and you should drift southwest.

Now think about trying to go *east.*

What if you tried to build the riskiest possible stock portfolio—the combination of stocks with the greatest possible instability of return from period to period?

Again, in the context of Figure 6.14, a deliberate attempt to move toward the east should be accompanied by a drift toward the north—toward higher return.

Attempt to go east, and you should drift northeast.

West by southwest; east by northeast. This is how it's *supposed* to be.

Now let's find out how it *is*.

FACT: WEST BY NORTHWEST; EAST BY SOUTHEAST

Let's try a simple experiment, using the historic record of stock returns.[7]

In building two simulated portfolios of stocks, we're going to alternately try heading west and east. No attempt will be made to raise or lower future return. We'll just build a portfolio we think should have very low volatility of return, as well as a portfolio that should have very high volatility.

And then we'll determine whether these portfolios subsequently produce relatively high or low returns.

To the north or to the south? That is the question.

We begin with stocks that are traded on The New York Stock Exchange.[8] We start the experiment all the way back in January, 1928. At the beginning of the first quarter of 1928, we find the combination of stocks (names and fractions of our money invested in each name) that would have produced the lowest possible volatility of return over the trailing 24 months (1926–27).

To insure that low volatility *in the past* will be roughly consistent with low volatility *in the future*, we need to keep our portfolio diversified. That is, we need to avoid plunging too deeply into any one stock or any one indus-

---

[7]The analysis of this chapter is joint work with Nardin Baker and the research team of National Investment Services of America, a money management firm based in Milwaukee, Wisconsin.

[8]The results are based on the monthly data files constructed by the Center for Research on Security Prices at the University of Chicago. These tapes are very clean and have little or no survival bias.

try. We also want to keep the composition of the portfolio relatively stable over time to avoid severe distortion of our results, as returns get eaten up by trading costs.

At the beginning of each quarter, we'll use Harry's Tool to find the portfolio with lowest possible *trailing* volatility,[9] subject to the following constraints:

1. No more than 5% of the portfolio can be invested in any one stock. The minimum is 0%. (Short selling is not permitted.)

2. No more than 20% of the portfolio can be invested in any one industry.

3. We can't invest in a stock more than 3 times its percentage of the market's total value. (If IBM constitutes 1.5% of the total market value of all NYSE stocks, we can't invest more than 4.5% of the portfolio in IBM.)

4. Turnover in the portfolio is constrained to 20%.[10]

From now on, we shall refer to these as *The Rules*.[11]

We'll buy and hold the portfolio we build until April, 1928. At the beginning of this next quarter, we'll once again build the portfolio which would have had the lowest volatility over the trailing 24 months, using all The Rules, including #4.

We continue doing this, quarter after quarter, until we reach the last quarter of 1992.

Then we'll see how our performance would have looked in the periods following portfolio construction.

---

[9]Volatility is defined as standard deviation of monthly return (calculated including dividends as well as capital gains). Using a numerical procedure, we are able to find an exact solution (given the weighting constraints) to the problem without having to invert the covariance matrix of returns.

[10]After considering the effects of trading on costs and expected volatility, trades are made until marginal trading costs per unit of reduced volatility reach a level consistent with 20% annual turnover in the portfolio.

[11]The results you are about to see are not very sensitive to changes in The Rules. Variations in The Rules have been independently tested by Barra, one of the largest vendors of financial technology in the world. Tests of the effect of varying The Rules are presented in Barra's first two newsletters of 1992. These can be obtained from Barra on request.

We will also follow The Rules in going east.

At the beginning of each quarter we build the portfolio with the *highest* trailing 24-month volatility of return. This portfolio is also held for each quarter and then reconfigured at the beginning of the next.

So—at the beginning of each quarter, we attempt to go west, and we attempt to go east.[12] We build two portfolios that we believe will have low and high volatility in the future.

And then we watch the portfolios to see what kind of returns they *subsequently* produce.[13]

The results of this experiment are presented in Figure 6.15.

Not what the MBAs expected!

The *low-volatility* strategy has *higher* realized return than the S&P 500, and the *high-volatility* strategy has *lower* return.

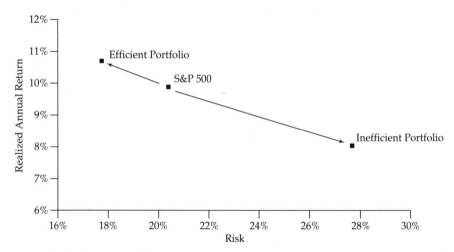

FIGURE 6.15. The effect of moving to lower- and higher-risk portfolios of NYSE stocks (1928–1992)

---

[12]There are undoubtedly better ways of going west and east than simply controlling trailing volatility. We use this technique because (a) it's easy to understand; (b) it's replicable by others; and (c) it works pretty well.

[13]As such, this is an out-of-sample test using information (past stock returns) that is available at the time of portfolio construction at the beginning of each quarter.

Notice that, in going west, no effort was made to find the stocks with the highest expected rates of return. And we weren't looking for the dregs, in going east, either. We were simply looking for the combinations of stocks with the lowest and highest volatility.

These results testify to a risk-return relationship that has been turned up-side down, with the lowest risk stocks producing the highest return.

Turned up-side down by a market that overreacts, overpricing growth stocks which *subsequently* have high volatility as investors' high hopes for the future are crushed by competitive forces and mean-reversion.

Turned up-side down by a market that overreacts, underpricing the unexciting value stocks which are characterized by low volatility.

The exciting, volatile growth stocks subsequently produce low returns; the dull, sedate value stocks subsequently produce high returns to the investors who bought them at bargain prices.

High risk—low future return. Low risk—high future return.

GO WEST YOUNG MAN (OLD MAN, BIG MAN, AND SMALL MAN)

The map is up-side down in the small as well as in the large.

The Frank Russell Company, a large investment consulting company, has constructed stock indexes that can be used as alternative benchmarks to the S&P 500.

Suppose you're a pension fund officer who wishes to assess the performance of a manager that only invests in small companies. There are many times that small stocks as a group over- or underperform the S&P. If you want to more accurately judge the skills of the manager in selecting good, small stocks, you may want to compare his or her returns to an index made up of small companies only.

To accommodate, Russell has constructed the Russell 1000 and the Russell 2000. The two indexes contain roughly the 1000 largest stocks and the next 2000 respectively. And it should be noted that the 2000 are all small companies.[14]

---

[14]The total market value of the common stock of the largest company in the Russell 2000 is currently approximately $200 million.

The Russell indexes have a history that begins in 1979, so we shall begin the next experiment in that year.[15]

As above, we shall use The Tool and The Rules to identify the portfolios with the lowest and highest levels of volatility of return in the previous 24 months. We do it at the beginning of each quarter, starting with 1979, hold the portfolios for a quarter and reconfigure at the beginning of the next.

The performance of the Russell 1000 and 2000 is shown in Figure 6.16 by the filled and unfilled squares labeled large- and small-firm stock indexes. As with the S&P 500, the rule used in constructing these indexes is to buy a common percentage of the total market value of each stock in the index. Thus, the percentages invested in each stock are proportional to the sizes of each company.

Note that in both cases our attempt to go west, to the efficient (low-volatility) versions of the Russell indexes, results in a drift north toward

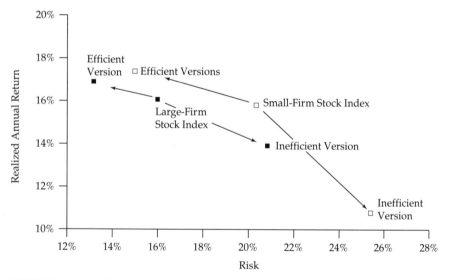

FIGURE 6.16. The effect of moving to lower- and higher-risk portfolios (1979–1992)

[15]In doing our tests, we used the actual composition of each of the Russell indexes at the beginning of each of the quarters, as obtained from the Frank Russell Company. Thus, our tests are completely free of survival bias.

higher return. Likewise, moving to the east, to the inefficient (high-volatility) versions, results in lower return.

Note also that the east-west as well as the north-south movements in Figure 6.4 are greater for the small stocks than for the large.

There are good reasons for this.

Addressing the greater east-west movement first, this can be explained by the fact that *small stocks have greater variety.* They have a wide range of individual volatilities. Their individual returns respond differentially to a wide range of different factors such as the price of oil, the rate of inflation, etc. This gives The Tool more room to work its magic in finding portfolios of very low risk and very high risk. Large stocks, on the other hand, are already "portfolios" or groups of different individual enterprises. Undeniably, there was a rationale for why they were assembled together, but it's not likely that the rationale had much to do with lowering stock volatility. Since The Tool can't disassemble the large companies for investment purposes, it's stuck with them, and this inhibits its power to control risk.

Now the greater north-south.

This happens because, within any population of stocks, *the risk-return tradeoff is truly negative.* The more you lower risk, the greater return becomes, and the more you raise risk, the lower it goes.

VALUE MAN AND GROWTH MAN TOO

Lowering volatility of return improves the performance of investment managers with different styles, such as those that want to invest in value stocks or growth stocks.

The Frank Russell Company has value indexes and growth indexes too.

To construct them, they take a stock population like the Russell 1000, rank the stocks by book value to market value, highest first, lowest last. Then they go down the list until there is equal total market value in the top half and the bottom. The top half becomes the value index, the bottom the growth. Other than that, the indexes are weighted like the S&P (based on size). The same process is used for the 2000 stocks in the small-firm population.

In Figure 6.17, we see the results of heading west and east from the large- and small-stock *value* indexes.[16]

Once again, we end up in the *northwest* and in the *southeast*.

In Figure 6.18, we try it for the growth stocks. Same answer.

Also, in both cases, bigger movements in the small than in the large.

Lowering volatility is even good for growth managers.

Most managers are primarily concerned with what they call their "buy list." On the buy list are the stocks they feel are good investments. Most managers give scant attention to the question: "How much money should I invest in each of the stocks on my buy list?" If anything, most think in terms of an equal amount in each stock.

Hardly anyone uses The Tool.

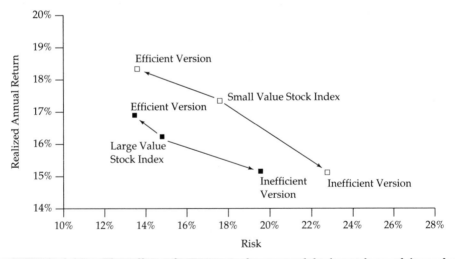

FIGURE 6.17. The effect of moving to lower- and higher-risk portfolios of large- and small-value stocks (1979–1992)

[16]At the time of the study, the Frank Russell Company had no small-cap growth and value indexes. Thus, we had to construct our own. In constructing the small stock growth and value indexes, we used the same rules that Russell applies to the large-cap growth and value indexes.

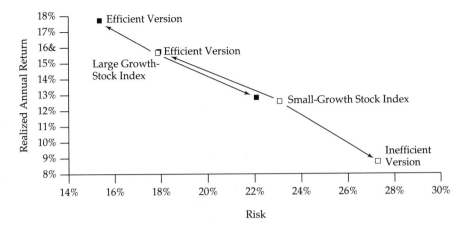

FIGURE 6.18. The effect of moving to lower- and higher-risk portfolios of large- and small-growth stocks (1979–1992)

They should.

They should *all* use it.[17]

They should help make CAPM come true.

They should give their buy lists to The Tool, and head directly for the west.

Well, not exactly *directly.*

They'll drift north some. Toward higher return and more stable performance.

Just like it works on Russell's lists of big, small, growth, and value companies, it should work on their buy lists.

Furniture makers have different styles too—Danish modern, French provincial, Colonial, etc. But they all do one last thing before they are finished making their furniture. One last step in the process. A step that makes their furniture at once more attractive and more durable.

[17]True, their clients may hold investments in addition to that which is vested by a particular professional manager. This being the case, the manager should optimize the portfolio under his or her discretion, while taking into account the statistical properties of the clients' other holdings.

They apply varnish.

Using The Tool to allocate funds across your buy list is like applying varnish to furniture.

It makes no difference to The Tool how you came up with your buy list. You don't have to change your investment process to use The Tool. The Tool will help to take you to the *North*west.

Stop trying to sell us *unfinished* portfolios!

FIVE-YEAR HORIZON TEST OF THE RELATIONSHIP BETWEEN RISK AND EXPECTED RETURN

In Figure 5.4, we saw the rolling 5-year relative performance of value vs. growth stock investing. There is a similar stability in the relative performance of low- vs. high-volatility stock portfolios.

This time we will work with the stocks in the S&P 500 stock index. To make sure we have no survival bias in our test, as with the tests above, we will use the S&P population that actually existed at the beginning of each quarter of our analysis.

We use the same procedures as above, but we extend the period to 1972 through 1992. Once again, at the beginning of each quarter, we use The Rules to compute the low-risk and high-risk portfolios based on the 24 monthly trailing returns.

Now we slide a 5-year window through all possible successive 20-quarter periods. In each of the periods we compute the realized return and volatility of return to each portfolio. Then we subtract from each the corresponding numbers of the S&P 500. In Figure 6.19, we plot the performance of both portfolios relative to the S&P 500. Higher realized return relative to the S&P is positioned above the horizontal axis; lower volatility is positioned to the left of the vertical.

As you can plainly see, the relative performance is *highly* consistent.

Within the context of a 5-year horizon assumption, there is little support for The Theory's prediction of a positive relationship between risk and return.

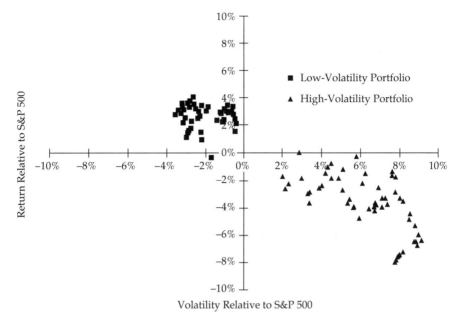

FIGURE 6.19. Test of 5-year horizon performance of low- and high-volatility portfolios using S&P 500 stocks (1972–1992)

THE HERETICS AND THE ZEALOTS FINALLY AGREE

Both the Heretics and the Zealots agree that The Theory should be abandoned. Both see the premium returns in value investing. The disagreement is over the nature of the premium—is it a surprise or a risk premium?

Both would agree that The Theory is wrong about the major market indexes being positioned in the vicinity of the efficient set. Both would agree that portfolios with lower volatility and higher return are attainable.

The argument centers on the nature of GO. Is it a surprise or is it a risk premium?

The Zealots argue that the premium to low-volatility portfolios stems from the fact that risk has a deeper meaning to investors. Risk goes beyond volatility—to the sensitivity of returns to a multiplicity of macroeconomic factors. Concern over these "higher" dimensions of risk transcends concerns about volatility.

There's something about the low-volatility portfolios that frightens us. There's something about the high-volatility portfolios that gives us comfort. We expect and require the differential returns on these portfolios.

So . . . they say.

It's not mispricing stemming from overreaction that creates systematic and predictable differences between what is *expected* and what is ultimately *received*. A pattern of mispricing that overrides our desire to get higher returns from high-volatility investments.

But . . . we say.

We *want* higher returns on high-volatility stock portfolios, but we don't *get* them because we overreact to the past and ultimately receive low returns in the future. We are afraid of volatility. We are *very* afraid.

This is why Edgar Lawrence Smith and many others find that stocks consistently outstrip bonds in their returns by such a wide margin.

We are afraid of stock volatility, and we demand very high returns to invest in stocks.

Our fear can also be seen in studies that transcend the cross-sectional distortion in relative stock prices caused by overreaction. These studies document the fact that we react very negatively to unexpected increases in the *overall* level of volatility in the market.[18]

As the volatility of the market index goes up, the *general level* of stock prices goes down so that higher returns can be earned in the future as we go through the period of higher volatility. And the returns do turn out to be higher *following* the price adjustment.

Conversely, unexpected drops in volatility are accompanied by increases in the level of stock prices as investors lower their required returns. And realized returns turn out to be relatively low following the price adjustment.

Our reactions to changes in volatility are strong, consistent, and significant.

[18]See, for example, French, K. R., G. W. Schwert, and R. Stambaugh, "Expected Stock Return and Volatility," *Journal of Financial Economics*, 1987, pp. 3–29. Also Haugen, R. A., E. Talmor, and W. Torous, "The Effect of Volatility Changes on the Level of Stock Prices and Subsequent Expected Returns," *The Journal of Finance*, 1991, pp. 137–158.

We *are* afraid of volatility.

But these fears don't show up in the cross-section of stock returns[19] because they are blurred and ultimately erased by market price distortions related to overreaction.

WHY YOU DON'T SEE THIS IN THE TEXTBOOKS

Maybe you have seen graphs in finance books showing a positive relationship between risk and expected return in the stock market.

Where did these results come from? Did somebody make them up?

To see what's been fooling us for so long, we need to go back to the Fama and French study of Chapter 1.

FF did some tests which extended over a longer period (1941–90). In these tests, NYSE stocks were ranked first by size during each year. The largest 10% of the stocks went into group #1, the next largest 10% into group #2, and so on. In each successive year the stocks were reranked and regrouped.[20]

Then the monthly returns to each of the groups are observed over the period 1941–90. The average returns to each group are plotted against their market sensitivity (beta) in Figure 6.20. The smallest stocks are to the upper right, and the stocks become progressively larger as we move to the lower left.

We see a positive tradeoff between risk and realized return.

This is what you're used to seeing.

---

[19]It has been argued (See Roll, R. and S. Ross, "On the Cross-Sectional Relation Between Expected Returns and Betas," Working Paper, May, 1992) that the cross-sectional results are merely the result of selecting an index that is not the true market portfolio. However, the betas computed with respect to this index do represent the contribution that the individual stocks make to the volatility of the index. Since other studies clearly show that investors react negatively to unexpected increases in the volatility of the U.S. stock index, how can it also be that the same investors who fear volatility in the index expect the lowest rates of return from the stocks that make the greatest contribution to that volatility? The answer seems to be that they do not *expect* the relatively low returns. They come as a *surprise*.
[20]The portfolios are equally weighted across the stocks.

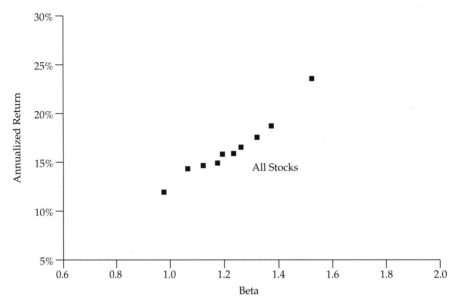

Source: Fama, E. and K. French, "The Cross-Section of Expected Stock Returns," *Journal of Finance,* Vol. 47, No. 2, Table AII.

FIGURE 6.20. **Beta versus return for size-formed portfolios (NYSE 1941–1990)**

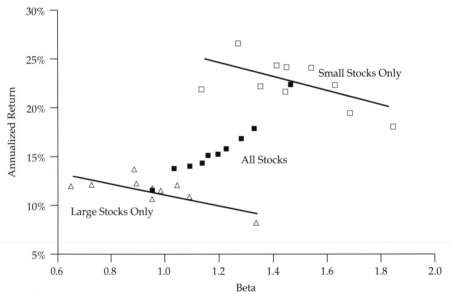

Source: Fama, E. and K. French, "The Cross-Section of Expected Stock Returns," *Journal of Finance,* Vol. 47, No. 2., Table AII.

FIGURE 6.21. **Beta versus return for large and small stocks (NYSE 1941–1990)**

But what we're seeing here is not a manifestation of a *risk premium*. In fact, it's a manifestation of a *size premium*. Small stocks carry bigger expected returns. They also tend to be riskier. But their superior returns are driven by size rather than by market risk.

To show this, FF now take each of their size groupings and rank the stocks in them by beta in each of the years. For the largest stocks, the 10% with the largest betas are placed in group #1a, the next 10% in group #1b, and so on. Then the monthly returns for each of the subgroups are observed over 1941–90, and beta is plotted against average return. If beta were the true driving factor behind the return differentials of Figure 6.9a, the subgroups should fill in the gaps between the large-stock grouping to the lower left and the smaller-stock groupings to the upper right.

As we can clearly see in Figure 6.21, they don't. The subgroupings appear as triangles. Within the largest stocks, those with highest risk tend to have the lowest returns. The line of the best fit passing through the subgroup scatter has a negative slope.[21] The same is true for the smallest stocks (the unshaded squares).[22]

High risk, low return.

GO west big man and small man.

What the text books tout as a risk effect is really a size effect.

---

[21]The negative relationship between risk and return for large stocks was first reported nearly 20 years ago in Haugen, R. A. and A. J. Heins, "Risk and the Rate of Return on Financial Assets: Some Old Wine in New Bottles," *Journal of Financial and Quantitative Analysis,* December, 1975, pp. 775–784. Given the nature of their sampling technique, HH unwittingly observe the relationship between risk and realized return for *large, established firms.* They find the relationship between risk (beta and volatility) and realized return negative and significant for equally weighted portfolios over the periods 1926–71, 1946–71 and various subperiods within.

[22]Size and beta are obviously highly correlated. This will cause a multicolinearity problem in all regressions where size and beta appear together, which will make it difficult to interpret the coefficients on each variable. In Jegadeesh, N., "Does Market Risk Really Explain the Size Effect," *The Journal of Financial and Quantitative Analysis,* September, 1992, pp 337–352, portfolios are constructed to minimize the collinearity between size and beta. In multiple regressions with both variables, Jegadeesh finds a significant size effect, but a negative (but nonsignificant) relationship between beta and realized monthly return over the period 1954 through 1989. Jegadeesh uses the CRISP database for his analysis, which is free from survival bias.

"V" IS FOR VICTORY

Investors do not expect risky stocks to produce lower returns. The low returns come as a surprise. Much is expected of these growth stocks in terms of future profitability.

Too much.

Mean reversion takes effect, and the actual performance is disappointing. As expectations are revised—returns on the risky growth stocks systematically turn out to be lower than expected.

High risk, low return.

If overreaction is behind the up-side down relationship between risk and return, we should see the relationship flip from right-side-up to up-side down *when the market initiates its tendency to overreact.*

As discussed in Chapter 3, the market had a relatively brief flirtation with growth stock investing in the late 1920s. During the 30s, 40s, and through most of the 50s, investing on the basis of projected growth was out of favor; instead, the prevailing investment philosophy was that exposed by Graham and Dodd in their book *Security Analysis.*[23]

In the final stages of the great bull market of the 1950s, growth stock investing made a comeback. Investing on the basis of projected future growth was once again accepted practice, and would remain as such *until this day.*

This gives us two interesting and distinguishable time periods. Growth stock investing has dominated over the past 35 years. The views of Graham and Dodd dominated over the 30-year period prior to that.

If this is true, we should be able to see the risk-return relationship flip up-side down following the comeback of growth stocks. The relationship between risk and return should be primarily positive during the first period and primarily negative during the second.

---

[23]Graham, B., and D. Dodd, *Security Analysis* (New York: McGraw Hill, 1934).

To see if this is the case, we shall examine the cumulative difference in performance between the low-volatility portfolio discussed earlier in the chapter and the S&P 500 stock index.

If overreaction is behind what we see in the data, we should observe a "V"-shaped pattern in the cumulative difference in performance.

In the era of Graham and Dodd, expectations should be realized, on average. Risky stocks should produce higher returns. Low-risk stocks should produce lower returns. The low-volatility portfolio should tend to underperform the market average.

The cumulative difference in performance between the low volatility portfolio and the S&P 500 should initially trend downward.

After the renaissance of growth stock investing, overreaction sets in. Expectations become biased. Growth stocks produce lower returns than expected. Low-volatility value stocks produce higher returns than expected.

The cumulative difference in performance should trend upward following the renaissance of growth stock investing.

Down, then up. We should look for a "V" shape in the historical record of cumulative relative performance. Let's see if we can find it.

The low-volatility portfolio will be constructed, at the beginning of each quarter, in accord with The Rules. At the beginning of each quarter, we will find the combination of all stocks listed on the New York Stock Exchange (because of our stock population and the nature of The Rules, we're going to be in the relatively large-stock segment of Figure 6.9a and 6.9b) that would have had the lowest possible volatility over the trailing 24 months. We will then hold this portfolio for the next quarter and then revise the weights according to The Rules.

Since we need two trailing years to compute the low-volatility portfolio weights, we can begin the experiment in 1928—two years after the beginning of the CRISP[24] tapes.

The cumulative difference between the return on the low-volatility portfolio and the S&P between 1928 and 1992 is plotted in Figure 6.22.

---

[24]Center for Research on Security Prices (University of Chicago).

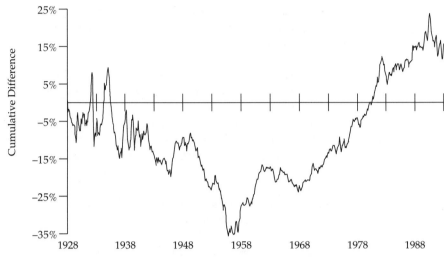

FIGURE 6.22. Cumulative difference in return between low-volatility portfolio and S&P 500

There it is!

Down during the era of Graham and Dodd. Up during the modern age of growth stock investing.

Note that the "V" points to 1958—*the time of the renaissance!*

Chapter Seven

THE HOLY GRAIL

RECAP

To see the big picture, let's bring together much of what we have learned so far.

A *value stock:* a stock for which earnings per share are expected to grow at a slower-than-average rate in the future.

A *growth stock:* a stock for which earnings per share are expected to grow at a faster-than-average rate in the future.

Today's market prices value and growth stocks as though they can be expected to distinguish themselves, in terms of their relative growth, for many years into the future.

The idea that relative growth can be forecasted for long periods into the future—growth stock investing—has been visited upon us twice in this century. Each time it came, no evidence was brought forth that long term future growth was, in fact, forecastable. Growth stock investing just came, went, then came back and stuck around.

In fact, because value companies tend to reorganize and reinvent themselves or are taken over and forced to do just that, and because growth companies face hungry competitors eager to participate in profitable product markets, the bad and the good become the average much faster than the market realizes (see Figures 4.1 through 4.5).

In the very short run, good earnings reports tend to be followed by a few more. This is also true of bad reports. The market is slow to react to the beginning of the chains. However, *after several links of the chains are in place, the market then overreacts,* thinking the chain of future positive (or negative) reports is apt to be a very long one. In reality, the subsequent links in the chain are equally likely to reflect above or below average earnings performance. For growth stocks, the *above average* reports that may come along are *expected*, so no significant positive price responses accompany their receipt. On the other hand, the *below average* reports are *unexpected*. Because they are, their receipt is accompanied by downward price adjustments. *As a class,* growth stocks subsequently produce poor returns for the unfortunate investors that bought them at inflated prices.

The opposite is true for value stocks—positive surprises and good returns as the bad firms of the past quickly revert to the average (see Figures 2.4A and 2.4B).

Because the market initially underreacts and then overreacts, we see evidence of the presence of *inertia patterns in the short term* and *reversal patterns in the long term.* These patterns show up in studies that compute various measures of volatility of return, where return is alternatively computed over weeks, months, and then years (see Figures 2.6 and 2.7).

In all long-term races between value and growth, *value wins* (see Figures 5.1 through 5.6). We should expect this is an overreactive market. However, it may also be that investors expect and require the higher returns on value stocks because they are believed to be risky. We choose to dismiss this alternative explanation for GO because (a) the "risk premium" seems *unbelievably large*[1] (see Figure 1.2), (b) value stocks have *lower market risk in a market that clearly fears volatility* (see Figure 1.3), and (c) there's a *peculiar time pattern in the receipt of GO* around earnings announcement days (see Figure 2.4A and 2.4B) and at the turn of the year (see Figure 5.7).

Since the low-risk, value stocks tend to produce high returns, and the high-risk, growth stocks tend to produce low returns, *the market's fear of risk is overridden by its overreaction to past earnings trend.* Investors want, and think they are going to get, higher returns on risky growth stocks. But, alas, based on their promising past performance, investors drive the prices of risky growth stocks up too high. They demand and expect much from these risky stocks, but *to their surprise,* actual results tend systematically to fall short of their expectations, and the risky growth stocks, as a class, tend to produce lower-than-average returns. The opposite is true for low-risk value stocks (see Figures 6.15 through 6.19).

The story, thus far, in a nutshell.

---

[1]The differential realized return between value and growth is approximately twice the realized differential between equities and Treasury Bills. Are we really to believe that investors perceive the risk differential between value and growth to be twice that of the differential between equities and Treasury Bills?

LOOKING DOWN THE ROADS TO DIAMOND HEAD
AND DIAMOND BAR

You may remember from Chapter 4 that the "judge" gave me permission to recall an exhibit from the "hot shots" (Figure 4.5). I'm going to exercise that privilege now.

Let's bring back The Christmas Tree, turn on its lights, and collect our presents!

Figure 4.5 showed the relative growth rates in earnings per share for stocks grouped on the basis of the ratio of earnings per share to market price per share. It showed that in the years *after* the ranking by this ratio, the group of stocks with the largest prices in relation to current earnings (growth stocks) grew faster than average and the group of stocks with the lowest prices grew slower than average.

However, as we move ahead to two, three, four, and five years after the rankings, the high- and low-priced stocks revert to the average in terms in their earnings growth.

Let's assume that Figure 4.5 is a fair and accurate representation of the extent to which relative growth mean reverts as you move into the future. If this is the case, can we say that the market is pricing stocks fairly with respect to this mean-reverting process now?

We will construct a sample of stocks as of mid-year 1993 using the same criterion as Fuller, Huberts and Levinson used.[2] We then rank the stocks on the basis of earnings per share to market price per share. The median average values for the 20% of the stocks with the smallest earnings/price ratio (growth) and the 20% with the largest earnings/price (value) are as follows:[3]

Group	Earnings price ratio
Lowest E/P (Growth)	2.36%
Highest E/P (Value)	8.38%

To keep the math simple, assume an average market price of $100 for each group. This gives us average current earnings per share of $2.36 for the growth stocks and $8.38 for the value stocks.

---

[2]See footnote 12 of Chapter 4.

[3]Much of this section is the result of joint work with Harindra de Silva of Analysis Group Inc. As with FHL, our groupings are industry-diversified in accord with their methodology.

Now we need a long-term, nominal growth rate *for an average stock* to which the growth and value stocks will eventually mean-revert. The nominal growth rate is the sum of the expected rate of inflation and the real rate of growth in inflation-adjusted dollars.

Since 1926 common stocks in the U.S. have produced a 9% real (inflation-adjusted) rate of return for investors. Currently, an average stock pays approximately 34% of returns as dividends, leaving 66% * 9% = 6% for real growth.

Now we need an estimate of long-term expected inflation. We'll assume 3%.[4]

Thus, our estimate of 6% for real growth in stockholder earnings plus our estimate of 3% in long-term inflation brings us to expected nominal growth for an average stock of 9%.

So we interpret the growth numbers on the horizontal axis of Figure 4.5 as growth rates relative to 9%. Thus, in the first year the earnings of the growth stocks can be expected to grow at 9% + 8.6% = 17.6% and the value stocks at 9% − 9.9% = −0.9%.

However, remember that the value stocks start at earnings of $8.38 vs. $2.36 for the growth stocks.

Assuming the value and growth groups will follow the pattern of the black and white bars respectively of Figure 4.5 in the years beyond 1993, we can expect to get the time series of future earnings per share shown in Figure 7.1. Given the initial lead held by the value stocks (higher first year earnings) and the mean-reverting tendency of earnings growth, *the growth stocks will never catch up.*

To find out what this means to our rates of return as stockholders, we must convert these earnings numbers into dividend numbers.

The stocks in the value and growth groupings have about the same percentages of earnings paid out as dividends (26% vs. 24% respectively). Assuming these pay-out percentages revert to the percentage for an average stock (34%) with the same speed as relative growth rates revert to average,

---

[4] At mid-year, 1993, the rate of inflation in consumer prices was running at slightly less than 3%.

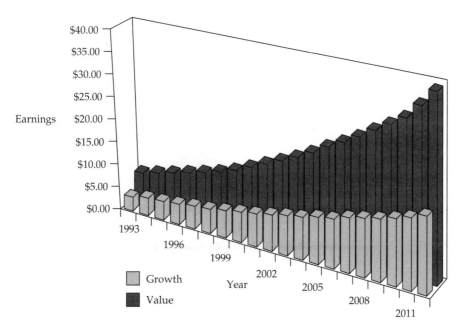

FIGURE 7.1. Projected earnings for growth and value stocks

we can expect to get the time series of future dividends in Figure 7.2. Again, the growth stocks will never catch up.

Let's assume we sell the value and growth stocks at mid-year 2013. At what price?

The median average earnings multiple (the ratio of market price to earnings per share) at mid-year 1993 was 18.24. Assuming that the present is the best guess for the future and recognizing that both the value and growth groups are likely to be viewed as average in 20 years, we apply this multiple to the 2013 values for earnings for the value and growth groups, and get:

2013 **Value:** 18.24 * $39.40 = **$718.94**

2013 **Growth:** 18.24 * $15.91 = **$290.20**

With bigger expected dividends and a higher expected selling price for the stocks in the value group, we must expect a higher future rate of return. We can calculate the expected future internal rate of return based on the future selling price, the dividends, and the current price of $100 for each group.

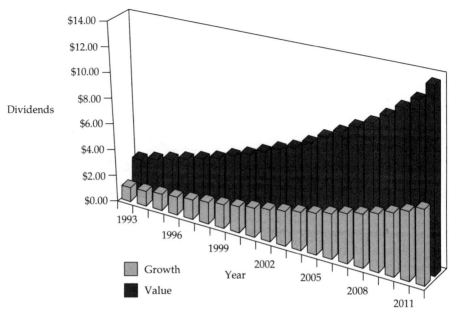

FIGURE 7.2. Projected dividends for growth and value stocks

The results:

Expected Future Return to Value: *12.64%*

Expected Future Return to Growth: *6.81%*

True, these differences aren't as large as the historical (1963–90) differences found by Fama and French (Figure 1.1) but remember that F&F looked at 10% groupings rather than the 20% groupings used here. Look at Figure 7.3. Here we plot the expected returns to all five groupings of stocks. To get a more reasonable comparison with the FF study we've split the two extreme groupings into equal parts (represented by the triangles) using linear extrapolation. The dark triangle to the extreme left represents an estimate of the expected return to the 10% of the stocks with the highest earnings-price ratios (expected future return equals 12.95%) at mid-year 1993. The light triangle to the extreme right shows an estimate of the expected return to the 10% of the stocks with the lowest earnings-price ratios (expected future return equals 5.99%).

In the FF study of the *history* of realized rates of return from 1963 through 1990, they found that the ratio of *realized* returns to value and growth stocks was 2.67 (21.4%/8%). Now looking forward rather than back

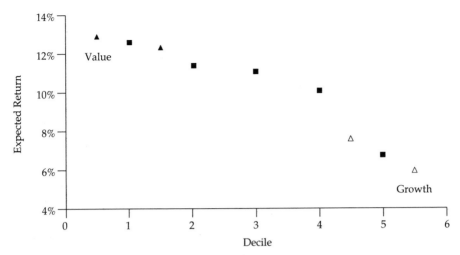

FIGURE 7.3. Expected returns through 2023

we find the ratio of *expected future* returns to value and growth to be 2.16 (12.95%/5.99%).[5]

From this we learn that *the forces that were in place to produce the relative returns to value and growth between 1963 and 1990 are still in place **to produce similar relative returns in the future.***

THE RELATIVE POSITION OF THE PERCEIVED AND TRUE GROWTH HORIZONS

Overall, the exercise of the previous section brings us to a simple but critical point:

> *Unless it reflects the presence of an enormous risk premium, the spread in the today's earnings/price ratios between value and growth (8.38% vs. 2.36%) is too large, given the strong tendency for earnings growth to mean-revert.*

---

[5]The difference in the ratios may be related to the fact that our groupings are industry-diversified while FF's were not, or they may be due, in part, to the fact that FF rebalanced their portfolios annually.

The wide spread in earnings/price ratios reflects the market's *perception* that investors can forecast relative growth rates in earnings for long periods into the future.

In Figure 7.4 we plot time into the future on the horizontal axis and growth in earnings relative to the average on the vertical. The growth rate of a stock initially expected to grow faster than average is represented by the solid line above the horizontal axis. For simplicity, we have assumed that the mean reversion takes place *suddenly* rather than *gradually*, as it actually does in Figure 4.5.

A value stock, expected to grow more slowly than average, is represented by the broken line of Figure 7.4. It is expected to mean-revert suddenly also, at the same time in the future as the growth stock.

Call the number of years until the perceived mean-reversion point the *perceived growth horizon.*

Note that, as the perceived horizon becomes longer, the relative market value of growth stocks becomes *larger* (faster than average growth for longer periods into the future) whereas the relative market value of value stocks becomes *smaller* (slower than average growth for an even longer period of time). Given current earnings and expected growth differentials, the longer the perceived growth horizon, the wider the spread in earnings/price ratios between value and growth.

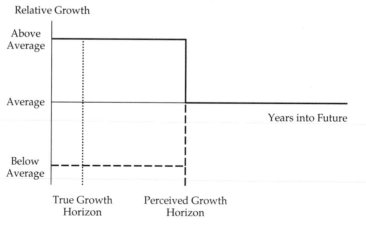

FIGURE 7.4. Perceived and actual growth horizons

The dotted line in Figure 7.4 represents the length of time we can *actually* forecast relative growth into the future.

Call the number of years until the true mean-reversion point the *true growth horizon*. In looking at Figure 4.5, and recalling the results of I. M. D. Little and others, we can safely say that the true growth horizon is relatively short. In the context of an assumed sudden shift as opposed to gradual decline, perhaps it is only two or three years out.

In this context, value stocks have higher future expected returns for two possible reasons:

1. The market is irrational and inefficient, and the perceived growth horizon is much longer than the true. Today's investors will be surprised at the differential in return when it is received. (This is the view of the Heretics.)[6]

2. The market is rational and efficient, and (accepting the results of Chapter 4) the perceived growth horizon is relatively short and, in fact, equal to the true. Today's investors are aware of the differential in the future expected returns to value and growth stocks. They believe value stocks are more risky, and they require the differential as a risk premium. (This is the view of the Zealots.)

The "old timers" of the Ancient Finance had a perceived growth horizon of zero years.

They didn't believe in taking future growth into account at all. This point of view was probably a little too extreme. Growth *is* forecastable, although for a rather short period into the future. On the other hand, the "hot shots" of the Ancient Finance and the growth stock investors of today have a perceived growth horizon as represented in Figure 7.4 *(assuming reason #1 is correct as stated above).*

We have made the case for reason #1 on the basis of *the timing of the receipt of the so-called risk premium* and the relatively *low market risk of value stocks.* However, there is another piece of anecdotal evidence that points to the conclusion that reason #1 is correct.

I think *they* know that Figure 7.4 is on target.

---

[6]This is discussed in R. Haugen, *Introductory Investment Theory* (Englewood Cliffs, NJ: Prentice Hall, 1987), pp. 422–29.

They are the managers of pension funds. I think *they* know because they are willing to hire *many* money managers of a particular type, and they hire *none* of the opposite type.

The type of manager they hire is called a "Bottom Fisher," one who sorts stocks on the basis of numbers that indicate cheapness in price. Bottom Fishers look for stocks with high ratios of earnings/price, dividend/price, book/market, etc. They don't pretent to have a "crystal ball." They don't consider the *future prospects* for a stock. They simply sort. They tout their disciplined approach to investing. They always buy and sell on the basis of their sorts. Emotions never come into play.

Pension sponsors willingly hire Bottom Fishers, even though they know they are working without crystal balls.

But the sponsors of today would never hire the *opposite* kind of manager.

These managers also invest without crystal balls. Don't consider prospects. Also sort. But these *"Rodeo Drive"*[7] managers go to the opposite side of the rankings. They look for stocks with *low* ratios of earnings/price, book/market, etc. They look for the stocks that are *the most expensive*, and they buy them.

As a consultant, if I were to advise a sponsor to hire such a manager, you can count on the fact that I would be laughed at and summarily fired!

*But such a manager would be expected to produce higher than average risk-adjusted returns if the perceived growth horizon were actually **shorter** than the true.* In such a world (pre-Edgar Lawrence Smith) the market would *underestimate the potential of growth stocks,* projecting above average growth rates for a shorter period than justified given the true level of mean reversion. In this world, the growth stocks would be systematically underpriced, and would subsequently produce superior returns for investors that bought them at bargain prices.

The "Bottom Fishers" can be expected to produce higher risk-adjusted returns, even without a crystal ball, only if the perceived horizon is longer than the true, as it is in Figure 7.4.

---

[7]Since managers like this don't really exist, I had to invent their name, based on one of the most expensive shopping areas known to man.

The fact that sponsors willingly hire "Bottom Fishers" and absolutely shun "Rodeo Drivers" implies that they sense that they are investing in an overreactive market. It seems that they realize that GO exists, but they don't reach for it.

Why?

Sponsors may be more concerned about keeping their jobs than they are about maximizing retirement benefits. They keep their jobs by matching the market, and this means hiring growth as well as value managers (the growth managers are purportedly armed with better crystal balls to help them overcome the relative positions of the perceived and true growth horizons).

As we learned in Chapter 5, growth stocks are big companies and, as such, they dominate the market averages. Shunning growth in favor of value means investing in a portfolio that can't be counted on to move in tandem with the market. Although you increase your odds of outperforming the market averages in the long run, you increase the probability of significant underperformance in the short run.

"If I reach for GO, it may cost me my job!"

It is important to know that *they* know.

Because they are so powerful in the market that, if they do reach for GO, it will disappear *for us*.

Without high levels of current wealth, we need the compounding effects of time to get to Diamond Head.

TWO COMPELLING QUESTIONS

The final case for GO requires answers to two compelling questions:

1. "Why hasn't all this been obvious before?"
2. "If the market is this inefficient, why do professional managers, as a group, generally underperform the market averages?"

One reason this has escaped the attention of the investing public is the very short horizons of the important players in the investment business. Pension sponsors pay very close attention to the performance of their managers. They are aided in this respect by the professional consulting industry. The standard of the consulting industry is to measure the performance of money managers over three trailing periods of time—the past year, the past three years, and the past five years.

Performance beyond the past five years is considered irrelevant because personnel and procedures employed by the money management firm in question have undoubtedly changed materially since then.

The studies that we have addressed in this book have been much longer term in nature. And it is only over the long term that the superiority of value investing becomes so obvious.

But there is another reason that may be even more important.

Consider the relative stability of the true and perceived growth horizons of Figure 7.4. The true horizon reflects the way the world actually is. This probability doesn't change very much over time. It is short because of the forces of competition and the propensity of below average firms to reorganize and reinvent themselves. Growth is relatively unpredictable now, and it has probably been that way for a long, long time.

We can't say the same about the *perceived* horizon, however.

We will go through periods where, by chance, the market will experience an unusually low number of earnings surprises. This result may strengthen the market's confidence in its ability to forecast relative growth. Following these periods stock prices may be restructured in a manner consistent with an *extension of the perceived growth horizon.* During these periods, the relative prices of growth stocks will go up. (Above average growth will be expected for even longer periods into the future.) The relative prices of value stocks will fall (below average growth for even longer periods). Growth will temporarily outperform value, as it did, for example, in 1990–91 (see Figure 5.4). *Periods such as these will serve to reinforce the notion that growth stock investing is a good idea.*

On the other hand, if we go through a period where there is an extraordinarily large number of earnings surprises, the market's confidence may be shaken and prices restructured in a manner consistent with a pulling back of the perceived growth horizon. In these times, the relative prices of value stocks will climb dramatically (with growth at below average rates for shorter periods than previously expected.)

As a result, GO does not come uniformly in time. In addition to its seasonal patterns (Figures 2.4A, 2.4B, and 5.7), *GO comes in "fits and starts" as the perceived growth horizon is extended and contracted.* Were it not for the instability in the perceived horizon, all of this would have been obvious a long time ago because it would have consistently shown up in the short-term analysis of performances that continuously goes on in the investment industry.

GO shows up so clearly in the long-term studies assessed here because *in the long-term it makes no difference whether the perceived growth horizon is unstable.* What counts in the long term is the average relative position of the two horizons. If the perceived is extended beyond the true, the cumulative return to value investing will gradually (but not steadily) climb relative to growth investing. But, given sufficient instability in the perceived horizon, it won't be obvious except to those who are concerned with relative performance *in the long run.*

What about the second question. *Why do money managers as a group consistently underperform?* In the past, their underperformance has been a source of inspiration for the Zealots. After all, professional managers are supposedly better informed. Why should they underperform *unless* they are facing an efficient market, where all stocks are correctly priced. Their underperformance was supposed to stem from a wasting of money on the search for nonexisting stocks that aren't correctly priced.

The problem with the Zealots' explanation is that managers, as a group, are often underperforming by *more than they could reasonably be expected to be spending on analysis.* This is hard for the Zealots to explain, because in an efficient market, it is just as difficult to find an overvalued stock to buy as it is to find an undervalued stock.

But the professional money managers often seem to be turning the trick![8]

And why should they want to?

Why should they want to invest in overvalued stocks?

Unless overvalued stocks are good-looking stocks. Stocks with good records of success. Stocks with good press. Stocks doing well. Stocks their clients will feel comfortable about having in their portfolios. Stocks that the market has overreacted to. Stocks that have risen in price too far. Stocks that

---

[8]See Lakonishok, J., A. Shleifer, and R. Vishny, "The Structure and Performance of the Money Management Industry," Brookings Papers: Macroeconomics, 1992, pp. 339–79.

will subsequently produce poor returns, *driving the performance of money managers as a group below the market averages.*

Why should they *not* want to invest in under-valued stocks? . . . Unless undervalued stocks are the ones with poor trailing records and bad press. Stocks their clients will feel uncomfortable about having in their portfolios. The ones with prices that have been driven down too far. The ones that will produce above average returns in the future.

"Remove them from the portfolio so we won't have to explain to our clients why they're there."

The reason managers underperform is *not* because they are facing an *efficient* market.

Managers underperform because they have an agency problem with their clients and, as a result, *they may be the **victims** of market inefficiency!*

BAAAAAAAAAH HUMBUG!

Even after reading this book you may want to entrust your money to a manager who invests in growth stocks. You should be willing to do this, however, only if you believe that the manager has a really clear and powerful crystal ball. Only if you believe he or she can find the growth stocks with truly great prospects. You should also make sure that this manager weighs carefully the price to be paid for those prospects.

But you should be aware of one major concern.

If the institutional investors lose faith in growth-stock investing and engage in a massive restructuring of their portfolios, *the consequences will be tremendous.*

Looking back at Figure 7.3, we see a wide gap between the growth and value extremes. If the institutional investors move to close that gap, woe to the investors in growth stocks. You may recall that the analysis of Figure 7.3 assumed a $100 current price for both growth and value.

The $100 price and the implied future cash flows gave us the differential expected rates of return, but *we can calculate the change in current relative prices required to give us the same expected future return to both growth and value.*

The growth stocks must fall in price from $100 to $41, and the value stocks must rise to $130.

If you invest in growth stocks you face a possible loss of almost 60% of your wealth *if the institutions move.*

Will they move?

Probably not.

Why?

The fiduciaries are sheep, and the portfolios managed by the flock all look pretty much the same: some cash, a little real-estate, a smattering of foreign stocks and bonds, a healthy chunk of domestic bonds, and a considerable commitment to domestic stocks. Most make a great effort (heartily endorsed by the professional consulting industry) to ensure that their stock investments are representative of the entire market—some growth stocks, some value stocks and some small stocks.

Why? Because their benchmark is the S&P 500. The S&P represents 90% of the total value of the market. And they don't want to be too different from their benchmark.

They don't want to act too differently from the other sheep.

They might stray from the flock and be eaten by the wolves that follow it.

They might underperform in the short run.

Let's take a closer look at the source of their fear. The source is a collection of laws called ERISA. Under it, fiduciaries can be sued and even face jail terms if they underperform and are found to have been *imprudent* in doing so. Corporate lawyers sit down with newly appointed pension officers and explain the perils of ERISA in clear and certain terms.

The pension officers then quickly appraise their position: they can lose, but they cannot win.

No one cares very much if they outperform the market. In fact, if they outperform by too much, they may be deemed guilty of taking unwarranted risk. They were imprudent, but lucky . . . this time.

On the other hand, if they underperform, eyebrows are raised. Continuation of this pattern for 3 years means likely termination. And *severe* underperformance can initiate real nightmares.

How can they keep from getting fired? How can they keep the nightmares from happening? By looking as much like the "other guys" as they can. By building portfolios that look as much like their cap-weighted benchmarks (the S&P 500) as possible.

A tremendous amount of money would have to be moved to drop the prices of growth stocks by 60%. And given the real fears of the fiduciaries, it's unlikely that nearly that much will be moved, at their peril, away from their cherished benchmarks.

The individual investor doesn't have these hang-ups. When did you last worry about *S&P 500 tracking error* in your personal portfolio?

Haven't given it a thought, have you?

We can reach for GO with impunity. And we will. And those of us who do will bury the institutional investors with our performance.

The fiduciaries are now and will be afraid to reach for GO.

GO is for *us!*

Chapter Eight

DAWN OF THE NEW FINANCE

The Fantasy is pervasive.

Open any contemporary text on the subject of corporate finance, and you will discover that it is written in the context of The Fantasy from beginning to end.

The objective function in corporate finance is to maximize shareholder wealth. We act in the context of this objective in setting standards for choosing the firm's investment projects (the cost of capital), in deciding how to raise money to finance those projects (the finance of the firm), and in deciding how to distribute cash flows from the projects to our stockholders (dividend policy).

In teaching us how to make each of these decisions, the underlying assumption of the text is that the firm's stock is priced in a rational and efficient market. And in most texts, the relative structure of stock prices is assumed to follow the dictates of The Theory (CAPM).

In this book we have learned that The Theory is a *highly inaccurate* depiction of reality. Moreover, the principal source of The Theory's failure is the failure of The Fantasy.

Given the truth of these statements, many of the principles of corporate finance need to be revised.

In this chapter we shall briefly review what those principles have been in the context of Modern Finance, and how they might be revised in the context of The New Finance.

117

THE COST OF CAPITAL

Firms calculate their cost of capital to make investment decisions. Most firms make decisions on the basis of their "average cost of capital." Since the firm obtains financing from different sources (common stock, debt, retained earnings, etc.), the firm estimates what its bondholders and stockholders require as a minimum return and then computes a weighted average of these returns, based on the relative amounts of debt and stock outstanding.[1]

In computing the required return on their stock, most firms assume that The Theory is correct. Why?

Because it's easy, and because they were taught it was the right thing to do in their MBA classes.

CAPM predicts that the expected rate of return on a firm's stock is given by the following equation:

*Expected Return = Risk-Free Rate + Market Risk Premium * Beta*

To show why CAPM makes it easy, let's go through a simple example. First you need a risk-free rate. If you're assessing the merits of a long-term investment project, you need a long-term cost of capital, so we begin with the expected return on a long-term government bond—say 6%.

Now we need a market risk premium. This is usually taken to be the average outperformance of the S&P 500 over long-term government bonds over the last 50 years or so—say 5%.

Now we need an estimate of our market sensitivity (beta). If we were truly ambitious we might go through the trouble of computing it ourselves, but most firms don't bother. They go to one of many sources that makes the computation (like Value Line[2]), and they use their number—say 1.5.

Now we're ready to do the arithmetic:

$$13.5\% = 6\% + (5\% * 1.5)$$

---

[1] In taking the average, the average must be adjusted to account for the fact that interest payments, but not dividends, are tax deductible for purposes of the corporate income tax. It should also be stressed that the weighted-average cost of capital should only be used to evaluate projects that are identical to the firm in risk characteristics and means of finance.

[2] The Value Line Investment Survey, New York: Value Line, Inc.

Pretty simple! But what good is it?

We know from the New Finance that a high risk stock like ours[3] can be expected to produce a lower-than-average rate of return. If the market's risk premium is 5% and the risk-free rate is 6%, the market's expected rate of return is 11%. Based on what we've seen, with our high level of risk, we should be coming in below that.

The Theory predicts that our stockholders expect 13.5% as a return on their stock. The Theory says that the number 13.5% should be averaged into our overall cost of capital.

This is wrong on two counts:

1. As we learned in Chapter 2, CAPM assumes we *all* use The Tool and invest in portfolios that occupy positions on the efficient set. If we do, "market beta" measures a stock's risk that is priced and the CAPM equation will describe our expected returns. However, it is almost literally true that *no one* uses The Tool to build his or her portfolios. This makes beta a poor measure of risk and the equation, itself, a sham. *Our stockholders' expectations* are unlikely to be fairly represented by The Theory's equation.

2. Surprisingly, except for *internal* equity financing, what we, as stockholders, expect isn't relevant. *What counts is what management expects.* And, in estimating the future return on the stock, they should employ the most advanced technology available to estimate the long-term future expected returns on their stock. They should then supplement this technology with their own *inside information* about the company's future prospects.

In making their investment decisions, all good managers should recognize that they always have a choice. They can (a) invest in the investment project, or (b) they can buy their stock back from their shareholders at the prevailing market place.

If they believe their own stock is a better investment than the project, they should shun the project and use the money to buy back their own stock. The stockholders that remain will be better off for it.

How is management to estimate the expected rate of return on its stock? Given the current state of the field, management probably should not

---

[3]The beta or market sensitivity of an average stock is 1.00. At 1.5 we are considerably more risky than average.

rely on theoretical models. However, inductive models exist which are capable of forecasting stock returns with significantly greater accuracy than predictions based on The Theory.

These models are called factor models, and they are designed to estimate and predict the influence of various "factors" on stock returns. The factors can be firm characteristics, like the size of the firm or its book-to-market ratio. We now know that firms of larger size usually have lower returns. The "payoff" to size is, therefore, usually negative. We also know that firms with larger ratios of book-to-market usually have higher returns. The payoff to the book-to-market factor is, therefore, usually positive. Factor models usually employ many factors like these. In using the models you must (a) determine the "exposure" of your firm to a particular factor (How big is it? What is its ratio of book-to-market?), and (b) project the payoff to each factor in the coming period. Your projection will probably be based on the monthly history of the factor payoffs. Some take the simple average of the past payoffs as their projection; others employ time series models.

Consider the following example.

Expected		*Expected*		*Estimated*		*Relative*
Stock	=	*S&P 500*	+	*Book/Market*	*	*Book/Market*
Return		*Market Return*		*Payoff*		*Exposure*

As in the CAPM example above, suppose management believes the expected return to the market will be 11% over the next two years. The book/market ratio for the S&P is found to be 0.7, while the value firm's ratio is 1.2. This means the firm's exposure to the book/market factor exceeds the market average. Its relative exposure to the book/market factor is $(1.2 - 0.7) = 0.5$.

Based on a past history of the cross-sectional relationship between realized returns and book/market ratios, management estimates the payoff to book/market to be 10%. This means that a stock with a book/price value of 2.00 can be expected to have a 10% greater return than a stock with a book/market ratio of 1.00.

Management's first cut at estimating the expected return on its stock is now:

$$16\% = 11\% + (10\% * 0.5)$$

It has recognized that it is a value company, and, as such, it carries a higher future expected return than the market. Now, the Zealots would say the 5% premium over the market is a *risk* premium that is expected by the firm's stockholders. Meanwhile, the Heretics would say that the premium in return is a product of overreaction and will be a surprise.

In this case it makes absolutely no difference who is right.[4] What the *stock-holders* expect is irrelevant. What counts is what *management* expects. And as a first cut, *they* now expect 16%.

As a second cut, they might want to add other factors to their model. For example, they might see size as an important determinant of expected stock return. The larger the company, the smaller the expected return. If they want to consider size, they need to add another term to the equation. This one will be the product of the estimated *payoff* to size (probably a negative number) and the relative exposure to size—size of the firm relative to the average size of firms in the S&P 500.

Now there are two components of the firm's expected return, relative to the S&P: the component coming from the firm's relative book/market ratio and the component coming from the firm's relative size.

Assume that the firm of our example is smaller than average, so taking this additional factor into account, the expected return estimate is raised to 18%. Management brings additional factors to the equation[5] until it is satisfied that its procedures for forecasting are state of the art.[6]

---

[4]Public utilities are generally considered to be low-risk firms and are regulated in accord with this view. They are allowed to earn relatively low rates of return on their invested assets, because their cost of equity capital is presumed to be relatively low. However, if these firms are actually low- (market) risk, value stocks, their expected returns may actually be quite large. Faced with the low returns allowed by the regulators, these firms might well choose to buy back as much of their undervalued stock as they can, and get out of the business as quickly as they can, while keeping their franchise to operate sunk investments. To prevent this from happening, the regulators have two choices. Allow higher rates of return, or acquire the utilities, and operate them as public agencies.

[5]Many contemporary factor models actually employed by investment professionals to estimate expected stock returns employ more than a hundred predictive factors.

[6]In estimating expected return with the model, the firm will want to consider the mean-reverting character of many of the factors. For example, if it is a value stock with a high book/price today, it is likely that this number will mean-revert in the future. The market's view of the firm's future prospects may become average or perhaps better than average. This being the case, the firm will want to estimate its relative *future* exposure to the book/price factor in each of the next n years, and then average the expected returns across the years to get its n-year expected rate of return.

The CAPM equation is *not* state of the art. It's an equation that comes from a theory of the way stocks are priced. *If The Theory is accurate,* we can use *it* to shortcut models like the one we are building in this example. *If The Theory is accurate,* once we build a model that is truly state of the art, we should find that our predictions conform to the predictions of the CAPM equation.

The different relative factor exposures that have non-zero expected pay-offs should all be related to risk and should all be subsumed in "beta."

But The Theory is wrong. And those who use the CAPM equation to compute the cost of capital are saving time that will ultimately cost their stockholders **dearly.**

Continuing with our example, *inside information* now comes into play. Management may *know* that they are not a typical value company. In the course of the next two years, they may be introducing several hot products (that presumably have sprung from different investment projects than the one being evaluated in this example) that are bound to change the stock market's assessment about their prospects. Based on this *inside* information, management believes that the expected rate of return on their stock over the next two years is a whopping 25%.

Now it must consider the risk of its stock relative to the investment with the 15% expected return. As a value company, its stock is relatively low risk. Since the project has lower return and higher risk, management should forego the project, and use the money to buy its stock back, unless it can find projects that are even better investments than the stock.

The stockholders that remain after the repurchase of shares will have their wealth appreciate because of management's decision.[7] *And it is they who will be casting votes at the next stockholders meeting!*[8]

---

[7]The trades associated with such a move should also exert upward pressure on your stock price. In addition, the act of buying back your stock may send a signal to the market that you feel the stock is undervalued. This signal may cause the market to revise its expectations as well as the price.

[8]In the context of the New Finance, and in a risk-neutral world, management should operate in the following general investment/financing decision framework. In considering the costs of raising capital through their firm, managers should employ state-of-the-art *inductive* technology (supplemented with their own inside information) to forecast the expected returns to their firm's menu of prospective securities. *Given the current state of the field, this technology should not be based on theoretical models.*

THE OPTIMAL FINANCE OF THE FIRM

The modern theory of the finance of the firm is also based on The Fantasy. To see how it works, let's assume we start a closed-end investment company.

A closed-end fund is similar to a mutual fund with one important difference. When you buy or sell the shares of a mutual fund, you buy and sell them from the mutual fund itself. Each day the total market value of the fund's investments is divided by the total number of shares outstanding, and that is the price you pay to get into or out of the fund.

A closed-end fund, on the other hand, sells a block of stock, just like a nonfinancial corporation might. This stock is then traded on the stock exchange. If you want to buy shares in the closed-end fund, you go to the exchange and buy them from someone who wants to sell them. You don't buy them from the fund itself.

---

*Rather, management should be confident that the technology is truly state of the art in terms of its power to predict future returns **out-of-sample**.* Next, management should determine the least expensive bundle of securities that can be issued. As we shall see in the next section, as long as the firm's assets are mis-priced by the market (over- or under-valued), the firm should be able to create security bundles that are *overvalued*. In finding the least expensive bundle, it matters not what the firm's security holders expected the returns to be or even what they want them to be. *What counts is what management believes they are going to be.* Next, management should consider their investment alternatives both in the real sector and in the financial sector. Remember, *in the inefficient market*, armed with state-of-the-art factor models, management may see investments with very high n-period rates of return in the financial markets. Management's own stock may be one of these, but it is special only in the context of management's private information and the fact that it is a tax-free investment. These n-period expected returns should be compared with the n-period alternatives in the real sector. In a tax-free risk-neutral world, assuming away attendant problems associated with mutually exclusive investments, issues of signaling, agency problems, and other factors that create interdependence between the investment and financing decision, management should opt for the investment with the highest expected return, *provided the returns are higher than the expected returns on the lowest-cost bundle of securities used to finance*. Management should continue its external financing and investing until the gap between the expected returns to the investments and the lowest cost sources of finance closes. For investments *internally* financed, management should accept projects that have expected returns greater than the greater of that expected by their existing stockholders or that expected on their stock by management itself. Following this path, stockholder wealth will be maximized.

Assume we start a closed-end fund. We begin by selling 10,000 shares of stock for $100 per share, raising $1 million. Immediately before doing anything with the cash, we check on our stock price and note that it is, as expected, still selling at $100.

For purposes of this example, assume that we can trade for free. Also *assume that The Fantasy is correct.* All securities trade in rational markets where they are fairly and accurately priced.

In thinking about the following transactions, assume they take place immediately. No time is allowed to elapse in between.

First, we take the $1 million in cash and buy blue-chip stocks with the money. We buy the stocks without trading costs, in a rational market, at fair prices. We check our stock price. Still $100, right? Right.

Okay, now we sell $500,000 worth of the blue chips, and we use the money to buy small stocks. No trading costs. We sell the blue chips at fair prices, and we buy the small stocks at fair prices. Again, we check our price. Still $100.

Why should it change? We're not adding or subtracting any value with these trades, and we're trading for free.

Another move. This time sell the rest of the blue chips, and use the money to buy corporate bonds. Check our price. It should still be $100.

We've been making these adjustments on the *asset* side of the balance sheet. Now we're going to shift to the right-hand side—which shows the *claims* to our assets.

All we've got there now is 10,000 shares of stock, each still worth $100.

Once again we're going to buy and sell fairly priced securities in the same efficient financial market. However, rather than buy and sell securities which are shown on the left-hand side of our balance sheet, *we're going to trade securities which are shown on the right-hand side.*

We sell $500,000 worth of (our own) fairly priced bonds in the market. And we use the money to buy 5,000 of our common shares back. Again, since we're buying and selling at fair prices, we neither create nor subtract value, so our firm should still be worth $1 million—5,000 shares of stock at $100 per share plus $500,000 in bond value.

Initially, we financed the purchase of the blue chips by selling common stocks. Now we've changed the structure of the financial claims to our asset portfolio to bonds as well as stock. But in doing so we had no effect on the total value of our firm because, just as with the fair trades we made on the left-hand side, we were unable to create value with the fair trades that we made on the right-hand side.

This is a rather simple explanation of the theory of the finance of the firm introduced in 1958 by Franco Modigliani and Merton Miller.[9] They showed that, in a rational and efficient market the total value of a firm (which pays no corporate income tax like our closed-end fund) is unaffected by the way it finances its investments. They also showed that taxable firms should favor debt because, for these firms, there are three different claims to the returns on the assets: (a) the stockholders, (b) the bondholders, and (c) the Internal Revenue Service. Since interest paid to the bondholders is tax deductible, increasing the amount of debt on the right-hand side of the balance sheet acts to reduce the value of the IRS claim, increasing the value of the other two. However, these arguments lean heavily on the notion that we trade at fair prices in a rational and efficient market.

If The Fantasy is correct, there is no optimal *investment policy* for our closed-end investment company, even on the asset side of our balance sheet. If all securities are fairly priced, we might as well have our portfolio manager throw darts at the Wall Street Journal to decide which securities to buy.

On the other hand, if the market is actually inefficient and overreactive, we have an optimal investment strategy. Fix our sights on Diamond Head, shun growth stocks, and invest in low volatility portfolios of value stocks.

Likewise, in an overreactive market, we're likely to have an optimal financing strategy on the *right-hand side* of our balance sheet.[10]

Suppose we're a value company, expected to grow at subaverage rates for a prolonged period. The overreactive market is undervaluing the assets of our firm. To finance our investments we can choose to issue undervalued stock or undervalued debt. In choosing, we should recognize that, because

[9]Modigliani, F., and M. Miller, "The Cost of Capital, Corporation Finance and the Theory of Investment," *American Economic Review*, June, 1958.
[10]As with actions taken to exploit mis-pricing on the left-hand side of the balance sheet, the benefits of financing optimally on the right-hand side will be reaped as the market corrects the mis-pricing of your securities.

of the fixed nature of their claim, the bonds will be less severely undervalued than the stock.

Holding other factors constant, as a general policy, we should favor
debt over equity financing. But not just any old debt.

In the New Finance, there will be an optimal term as well as an optimal
form of the debt we issue.

To see this, consider how we can actually benefit from the mis-pricing
of our bonds through the use of options which may truncate the life of the
bonds.

We can make the bonds callable. This means that we (management act-
ing in the interests of our stockholders) hold an option to buy the bonds
back at a stated price between an initial point in time, where the bonds first
become callable and the maturity date.

The value of this call option rises and falls with the value of the bond
that we issue.

In Figure 8.1 we plot the value of the (noncallable) bond on the horizontal axis and the value of a call option written on the bond on the vertical
axis. The curve shows the path that the value of the call option would take
as the value of the underlying bond increases.[11] As managers of the undervalued firm, we feel our bond is worth $1050, as given by the broken line.
Given this opinion, *we* would place a value of $269 on the option. The mar-
ket, however, believes the bond is worth $1000, as given by the dotted line.
As such, it values the option less than we do, at $230.

---

[11]The curve is drawn in the context of a standard binomial option pricing model,
where the exercise price is assumed to be $1050, the volatility is 10%, and the term to
maturity is assumed to be 5 years. Strictly speaking the standard binomial model is
inappropriate for valuing bond options for reasons that include the following: (a) it
assumes that the option can be exercised at a single fixed price at any time on or
before maturity; (b) it assumes that the returns on the underlying asset are normally
distributed, whereas the bond's returns are actually truncated because of the fixed
nature of its claim, and because the bond's yield-to-maturity can't fall below zero; (c)
the binomial model assumes that the value of the underlying asset is unaffected by
the existence of the option; and (d) the variance of the returns on the bond is not constant over time, but instead it falls as the bond approaches maturity. In spite of these
details, the arguments behind Figure 8.1 remain generally valid.

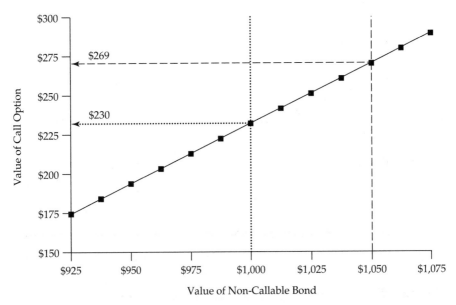

FIGURE 8.1. Value of call option on bond of a value stock

If we choose to sell a noncallable bond, we must sell it at $50 below its fair value. If, on the other hand, we sell a callable bond, we actually issue a package. *The bondholders* take a positive position in a noncallable bond (underpriced by $50) and a negative position in a call option on that bond (underpriced by $39). *We* take a negative position in the noncallable bond and a positive position in the call option. The net package is undervalued by only $11.

But we don't have to stop here. Figure 8.2 shows the value of a put option to sell the bond at a fixed price.[12] Note that an option to *sell* at a fixed price increases in value as the price of the underlying asset (in this case the noncallable bond) declines. In the case of our undervalued firm, the put option is actually overvalued because the market is undervaluing the bond it is written on. It would, therefore, be in our interests to attach this overvalued put to the undervalued bond and sell it as a package.

---

[12]The exercise price is again assumed to be $1050, the term to maturity 5 years, and the volatility of the bond 10%. The same caveats which we discussed for the call option also apply to the put option.

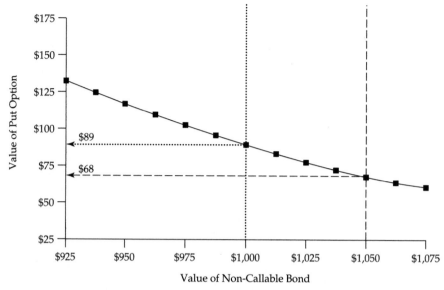

FIGURE 8.2. Value of put option on bond of a value stock

It is in our interests to make the bond both callable (we can buy it back from the bondholders at a fixed price) and put-able (the bondholders can turn it back to us at a fixed price). By adjusting the terms on the put and the call, we can eliminate undervaluation of the package, and actually turn a market disadvantage into an advantage.

Knowing our firm is worth more than the market thinks, we willingly sell an overvalued right to sell the bonds of our firm at a fixed price, and we are eager to hold, ourselves, a right to buy them back at a fixed price.

Similar arguments can be made for an *overvalued* growth stock.

Faced first with a choice of selling stock or bonds, the market overvaluation provides an incentive for selling stock. If, for other reasons (perhaps the tax advantage), you want to issue debt, you would want to avoid callable and put-able bonds. You would, however, favor convertible bonds, where the bondholders again buy a package—(a) an overvalued conventional bond and (b) an overvalued option to buy your overvalued stock. *Management* may also wish to hold an undervalued put option to sell more debt at a fixed price. They can avail themselves of such an opportunity by establishing a line of credit at say "prime plus" with a bank.

In the context of the New Finance, there is clearly an optimal capital structure as well as an optimal form of the financial contracts issued by the firm.

Firms apparently do make capital structure decisions based on perceptions of mis-pricing of their stock by the market. A recent paper by Loughran and Ritter (LR)[13] shows that the shares of firms that issue stock are, in general, overpriced, and subsequently these shares produce relatively poor rates of return.

LR observe 3,702 seasoned equity offerings in the period 1970–90.[14] They follow the performance of the shares from the date of the offering to five years thereafter.[15]

Figure 8.3 shows the results year by year for the 5-year period following issuance. The returns to the shares of firms issuing stock at the beginning of the first year are shown in the front row. The returns to "matching firms" with the same market capitalization as the issuing firms,[16] but which issued no new shares during the 5-year period that preceded the beginning of the first year, are shown in the back row.

Note that the returns to the issuing firms' shares are very low (with a geometric mean of 5.1%), and that the matching firms outperform in every year relative to the issue date.

It is fairly obvious from these results that the managers of these firms, as a class, knew that their stocks were overpriced and would, therefore, produce low rates of return in the future. This opinion may have been based on inside information.

Nevertheless, *an efficient market would have taken the announcement of an offering as a signal of management's opinions about the shares.* In an efficient market the prices of the shares should have fallen at the time of the

---

[13]Loughran, T. and J. Ritter, "The Timing and Subsequent Performance of New Issues," Working Paper, University of Illinois at Urbana-Champaign (November 29, 1993).
[14]All of the offerings involved at least some newly-issued (primary) shares. Public utility offerings were excluded from their sample.
[15]Actually the shares are followed up to the earliest of (a) the fifth-year anniversary of the offering, (b) the time the firm is de-listed, or (c) the end of 1992.
[16]To find a capitalization-matched firm, firms which did not issue stock in the 5-year period preceding the issuing data are candidates. The matching firm, in each case, is the firm with closest (but higher than) market capitalization to the issuing firm.

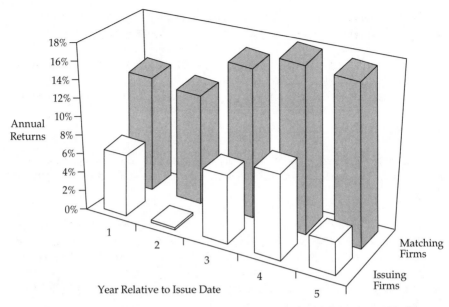

Source: Loughran, T. and J. Ritter, "The Timing and Subsequent Performance of New Issues," Working Paper, University of Illinois at Urbana-Champaign, Table IV.

FIGURE 8.3. Returns by year following issue for issuing and matching firms

announcement, and subsequent to the price-adjustment, the performance of the shares should have matched their benchmarks. Instead, Figure 8.3 reveals the tracks of an *inefficient* market that doesn't understand the implications of managements' issuing announcement. The negative price-adjustment doesn't take place at the time of the announcement. Instead, it takes place over the next five years, *as what management sees initially gradually becomes apparent to everyone.*

In Figure 8.4 the results of LR's study are separated by year. The figure plots the 5-year difference in the returns of the issuing firms and the matching firms.

LR find that, in 17 out of the 21 issuing years in their sample period (1970–90), the matching firms outperform in the following 5-year period, and in the 4 years that are the exceptions, the performance is nearly identical.[17]

We are obviously dealing with a persistent pattern that is quite robust with respect to most time periods.

---

[17]LR find very similar results for companies going public with initial public offerings.

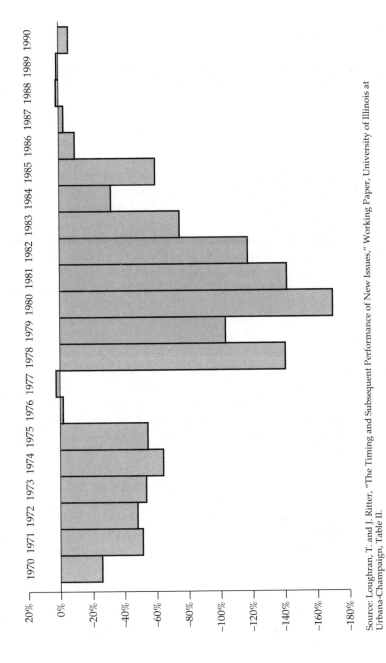

Source: Loughran, T. and J. Ritter, "The Timing and Subsequent Performance of New Issues," Working Paper, University of Illinois at Urbana-Champaign, Table II.

FIGURE 8.4. Subsequent difference in 5-year returns between issuing firms and matching firms (by year: 1970–1990)

DIVIDEND POLICY

Dividend policy addresses the question of how to optimally get the cash flows produced by the firm to its stockholders. There are two choices:

1. Write checks and pay cash dividends.
2. Write checks and repurchase your stock.

Dividend policy concerns the choice of paying fewer cash dividends and repurchasing more of your stock or paying more dividends and buying less (or perhaps even selling more) of your stock. Consider the effects of the choice on your stockholders.

If you pay more dividends, stockholders receive cash. They can use the cash to reinvest in your stock or the stock of any other firm. However, they must first pay taxes on the cash they have received. They also must incur trading costs in reinvesting the cash.

If you pay fewer dividends and, instead, use the money to repurchase your shares, *you* incur trading costs. Your remaining stockholders receive less cash and pay fewer taxes.[18] The market value of their shares goes up because remaining stockholders share the future cash flows of the firm with fewer fellow stockholders. In fact, our friends MM showed that, before taxes, stockholders end up with the same amount of wealth if dividends are paid or, alternatively, if shares are repurchased—*in a rational and efficient market.*

But what if you are a growth stock, and you know that your stock is overvalued. Why would you want to buy your overvalued stock? Would your stockholders not be ultimately better off if you used the funds to pay dividends or perhaps purchase the shares of other undervalued value stocks?[19] They would.

---

[18]It is possible that the IRS will recognize a systematic repurchase plan as a distribution of dividends and tax the distribution accordingly. There has been no precedent for this, thus far, however, for publicly traded firms.

[19]This can be done by making cash contributions to your pension plan, if they are allowable by the IRS, and then investing in value stocks within the plan. In this way you can avoid the corporate income tax on the investment income from the stocks. The surplus in the plan produced by such a strategy can be accessed over time by subsequent lower required contributions to the plan.

Holding other factors constant, the managers of *growth* stocks should favor cash dividends, and should avoid stock repurchase programs. The managers of *value* stocks should actively engage in repurchase programs.

And they should *time* their repurchases.

Factor models, like the one discussed in the first section of this chapter, can be used to predict the *short-term* return on your stock. For example, suppose you have just reported a positive "earnings surprise." You know that a few more good reports are on the way, but in its typical fashion, the market hasn't caught on to this yet. You estimate that the expected return on your stock is unusually high for the next year. This being the case, it is in your interests to repurchase an unusually large amount of your stock in the current period.

A recent paper by Ikenberry, Lakonishok, and Vermaelen[20] (ILV) reveals some very interesting facts about the subsequent performance of shares repurchased by firms. ILV observe a large sample of firms that publicly announced the intent to repurchase more than 1% of their shares in the open market during the 1980s.[21] They adjust the returns of the firms in their sample for the size and for the book-to-market factors that we now know have a significant influence on stock returns.[22] The average cumulative monthly returns from 36 months prior to the share-repurchase announcement to 48 months following the announcement are shown in Figure 8.5.

An interesting pattern emerges.

Of course, common to all the firms averaged is that they announced the intent to repurchase at month 0. This news was taken as positive by the market because the return was positive in the month of the announcement

---

[20]Ikenberry, D., J. Lakonishok, and T. Vermaelen, "Market Underreaction to Open Market Share Repurchases," Working Paper, University of Illinois, October, 1993.

[21]ILV look at a sample of 1,239 announcements over the time period 1980 through 1990.

[22]In making the adjustment ILV first rank their firms by total market capitalization each year. They form the firms into equally-weighted deciles. Next, within each decile, they rank by the ratio of book-to-market in April of each year, using the book value number for the previous year. Each size group is formed into quintiles based on book-to-market ratio. That gives them 50 equally-weighted index portfolios stratified by size and book-to-market ratio. In adjusting the monthly returns for a particular stock, they subtract from the stock's return the monthly return to the index portfolio to which the stock belongs. These net returns are represented in Figures 8.3 and 8.4.

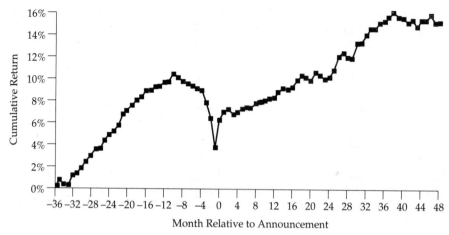

Source: Ikenberry, D., J. Lakonishok, and T. Vermaelen, "Market Underreaction to Open Market Share Repurchases," Working Paper, October 1993.

FIGURE 8.5. Size and book-to-market adjusted cumulative return to stocks announcing stock repurchase at month zero

but not in the month before. Apparently, neither the information about the intent to repurchase had leaked in advance of the public announcement nor had the repurchases already been started. Note that, on average, the stocks of these firms were falling in price during the nine months prior to the announcement. Interestingly, in the 27 months before that, the stocks were doing better than other stocks in their size and book-to-price class. We may be seeing here further support for the *long-run reversal* patterns documented in Chapter 2.

The peculiar pattern may also reflect a tendency for managers that have seen substantial fractions of *previous* gains *recently* wiped out to see their firm's stock as undervalued. Other firms that have been the victims of *prolonged* declines in their stock prices may have similar opinions, but they may be reluctant to repurchase because they wish to avoid further reductions in their equity base.

In any case, as ILV point out, the market's reaction to the repurchase announcement is apparently incomplete. Many of these firms were buying their stock back because they thought it was underpriced. *An efficient market would have recognized this signal, and the cumulative return should have moved to approximately 16% at month 0.* It does not. Instead, management turns out to be correct in its assessment, and the companies outperform their respective size and book-to-market benchmarks in the period following the announcement.

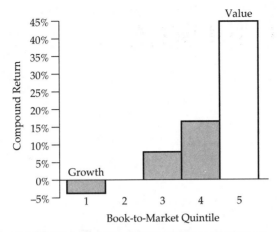

Source: Ikenberry, D., J. Lakonishok, and T. Vermaelen, "Market Underreaction in Open Market Share Repurchases," Working Paper, October 1993.

FIGURE 8.6. Compound four-year holding period returns for stocks announcing stock repurchases (ranked on book-to-market ratios)

Not all the companies announcing the intent to repurchase did so because they thought their stocks were underpriced. It's doubtful whether, *in general*, the managers of the growth stocks thought that the market had undervalued their stocks. These managers may have been motivated by other things, like getting cash flows to their stockholders in a way that minimizes the tax bite or by avoiding takeovers.

ILV now rank the firms in their sample on the basis of their book-to-market ratio in the year of the announcement. The cumulative returns between the announcement month and 48 months later are shown in Figure 8.6. Note that the value stocks outperformed their respective size and book-to-market benchmarks, but *no such tendency exists for the growth stocks*. Figure 8.6 clearly indicates that share-repurchase decisions by value companies are motivated by managerial perceptions that the market has underpriced their stock. Since they subsequently outperform their benchmarks, these perceptions seem to be driven by insider information that goes beyond their low book-to-market ratios.

In any case the *pathetically inefficient market* doesn't seem to have a clue as to what is going on.

Chapter Nine

FINAL WORDS

Finance scholars have long embraced the notion that we advance faster and better by *first* creating theories that make predictions about the way the world works. *Next* we turn to the data to see if the numbers conform to the predictions. If we find that they do not, we either (a) "refine" the theories, by altering the assumptions upon which they are based, or (b) "refine" the empirical tests until the data speaks in a voice we can *appreciate and understand.*

The Theory springs from the notion, "What would the world look like if we *all* used The Tool?" The origins of The Fantasy stem from (a) initial reports that successive percentage changes in the prices of large stocks appeared to be uncorrelated and (b) an understanding that, if security prices accurately reflected the available information set, they should follow a random walk. We spent the next thirty years bending and twisting first the data and then the theories, trying to make them sing in harmony.

But most of the major advances in the frontier of human knowledge did not follow an arrow running through the theories into the empirical tests. Rather, *most of our greatest triumphs proceeded in the opposite direction from data to theory.* The arrow goes from straightforward empirical observation to the development of theories which give us the insights *to understand what we have seen.*

In 1887, Michelson and Morley projected beams of light into directions that were different relative to the direction of the earth's orbital velocity. They expected to find that the beam cast *with* the earth's movement would move with greater speed than the beam cast *against.* To their surprise, they found that both moved with exactly the same speed. This empirical result inspired a young physicist named Albert Einstein to reconsider the laws of nature, given that the cosmos is bound by a universal speed limit—the speed of light.

In the 1920s an astronomer named Edwin P. Hubble spent many years atop Mt. Wilson peering through the 100-inch Hooker reflector. Hubble painstakingly made recordings of the magnitudes of the red-shifts in the spectrums of thousands of galaxies. After the years of straight-forward observations, he drew a generalization. The more distant a galaxy was from the earth, the more its spectrum was shifted to the red. Since the magnitude of the red-shift revealed the speed with which an object was moving away from an observer, Hubble drew the inference that the universe must be expanding.[1] Hubble's observations were passed to the astrophysicists. These theorists then crafted models (based on the common principle that the universe emerged in a momentous explosion from a singularity) that arguably stand as the greatest single intellectual advancement in the history of mankind.

From "How does the world work?" to "Why does it work that way?"

We have now seen the results of many straightforward attempts to document the behavior of stock prices. These results do not conform to the predictions of the theories. *They don't even come close.*

We in finance—did we not embrace our theories too quickly? Before learning how financial markets behave? Do we not embrace them now too tenaciously in the face of growing evidence that our fidelity is unfounded?

Who will now stand to deny the validity of the following statement: *"If, from the beginning, we knew what we know now, neither The Theory nor The Fantasy would have been offered for our serious consideration."* If we agree with this statement, would we not also agree that it is time to discard these long-standing paradigms of Modern Finance?

In the course of the past 10 years, financial economists have been struggling to explain the magnitude of the premium to equities relative to Treasury bills in the context of models based on rational economic behavior. This body of literature has come to be known as the Equity Premium Puzzle.[2] The struggle to explain the equity premium has been difficult. But it pales in comparison to the task of explaining the *huge, predictable premiums in the cross-section of equity returns.*

---

[1] Draw points on a balloon, and then blow it up. From the vantage of any one point, it will appear that all the other points are moving away, and the further away, the faster they will be moving.
[2] See Mehra, R. and E. Prescott. "The Equity Premium: A Puzzle," *The Journal of Monetary Economics* 2:145–161, 1985.

We have two choices. We can *advance* by developing radically new theories to help us understand what we now see in the data. Or we can *go back*, denying what is now readily apparent to most, bending the data through ever more convoluted econometric processes, *until it screams its compliance with our preconceptions.*

•   •   •

In Greek times, a scientist named Ptolemy devised a theory that was able to explain the observed movements of the stars and the planets. In Ptolemy's theory, the earth occupied the center of the universe.

The Roman Catholic Church embraced Ptolemy's ideas. After all, if man was made in God's image, why shouldn't he reside at a prestigous place like Universe Center?

But in 1576, a man named Tycho Brahe began the construction of an observatory, called the Castle of the Heavens. Tycho observed the movements of the heavens with instruments that were the best of his time. He measured and recorded the positions of 777 stars, and it is said his star positions were never in error by more than one or two minutes of arc.

It became increasingly clear that Tycho's careful observations were inconsistent with Ptolemy's theory. With the support of the church, mathematicians and scientists labored furiously to create new versions of Ptolemy's model, making it increasingly complicated so it would comply with the latest recorded observations.

Eventually, Brahe was joined by a younger man named Johannes Kepler. Kepler had studied the works of an earlier astronomer, Copernicus, and he realized that if he assumed that the earth, together with the rest of the planets, moved around the sun, most of the complications could be removed with one stroke. Kepler realized that, in science, a straightforward theory is usually more accurate than a more cumbersome one. In breaking with the doctrine of the Church, Kepler was able to develop a simpler theory with much greater predictive power centered on his three laws of planetary motion.

It is not clear whether any of the true believers in the earth-centered universe were ever persuaded by Copernicus, Brahe, or Kepler to change their minds. All may have gone to their graves still searching for further, more complicated versions of their model that would make it consistent with the latest empirical observations.

True believers to the last.

• • •

May we both spend our final years on the warm sands of Waikiki Beach.

Don't be afraid of the journey to Diamond Head.

You will find it to be a safe and comfortable one.

GLOSSARY

Bottom Fisher: Money manager, with no crystal ball, who favors stocks selling at the lowest prices relative to current cash flows.

Christmas Tree: The pattern of mean reversion in relative earnings growth rates.

Crystal Ball: Technology (subjective or quantitative) used to assess future prospects.

Diamond Bar: Retirement destination for an investor in growth stocks.

Diamond Head: Retirement destination for an investor in value stocks.

The Fantasy: Belief that stock prices always adjust to reflect the appearance of new and relevant information in an instantaneous and unbiased manner.

GO: The golden opportunity to go to Diamond Head rather than Diamond Bar.

Growth Train #1: Revision in standards for valuing stocks that occurred in the late 1920s.

Growth Train #2: Revision in standards for valuing stocks that occurred in the early 1960s.

Heretic: A disbeliever in The Theory and The Fantasy.

Hot Shots: Believers, in the late 1920s, in the new standards for valuing growth stocks.

New Finance: Belief that both The Theory and The Fantasy are wrong and that financial problems should be addressed with technology based on empirical estimation rather than theoretical constructs.

Rodeo Driver: Money manager, with no crystal ball, who favors stocks selling at the highest prices relative to current cash flows.

The Theory: (*alias* CAPM, SLM, SLB, SLFB, and so forth) Belief that all investors hold portfolios that have mean-variance properties consistent with those found with The Tool.

Old Timers: Disbelievers, in the late 1920s, in the new standards for growth stocks.

The Tool: Procedure to find the portfolios with the lowest possible volatility of return given an objective for expected return.

Zealot: A believer in The Theory or The Fantasy or both.

INDEX

Page numbers followed by *f* indicate figures.